THE ANCHOR

THE ANCHOR

ANALYZE THE SEASONS OF YOUR LIFE.
IMPACT GENERATIONS.

MIKE HARVEY

To my dad and mom,
I am what I am today because of you. Thank you for your
investment in me. I love you.

To my wife,
It is true: husband and wife become one. May this story bless
you as you see the impact you have had on my life. I love you.

To my kids,
May you fall in love with the Bible, which will lead you to
falling in love with your Savior. I would die for you. Love
y'all.

A message from the author:

GRACE /grās/: Undeserved complete forgiveness.

To me, the most beautiful word in the Bible is grace. You hold in your hands my life story. I ask for grace.

First, for the inevitable writing errors you will find. I had the book professionally and personally edited too many times to count, but, as an author friend told me, there will be errors no doubt. However, rather than more editing, I felt the need to get the book out.

Second, for the potential inaccuracies of the many stories that I tell. These stories are how I remember them. I may have some of the details off, so I ask for grace. It is tough to write years and years of memories.

Lastly, I ask for grace as you view life from my perspective. The world is as divided today as I have ever seen it. Grace is the one unifier we have at our disposal. I must regularly "reach across the aisle" and understand counter views of the way I view the world. And, grace must follow the differences.

I believe the message of The Anchor is needed now more than ever in my lifetime. COVID-19 has caused great fear and anxiousness in many lives. I pray The Anchor helps that one person who may need the message.

Thanks for reading and sharing.

PURPOSE:

Humbly share the God of the Bible through my story and inspire others to reflect and write about their unique journey, impacting family, friends, and future generations.

It happened at 5:00 AM on a random morning. My dad's life suddenly ended and with it a lost opportunity to record his life for future generations. I never took the time to interview him or record his life story. I vowed that my kids would have my story.

So, I originally wrote The Anchor for my kids. I want to inspire them, have them learn from my mistakes, give them life lessons, and, ultimately, give them the gift of their dad's story.

Years later, I decided to inspire others to do the same. I know few will embark in writing a book, but my hope is that the format of thinking through your life in seasons will give you an outline, at a minimum, to record your thoughts and inspire others.

Many parts of your story may be too painful to write. I found that out as I wrote about my journey. Additionally, some may never feel comfortable sharing parts of their story with their kids, much less generations. I understand that as well. In fact, I originally had two versions of the book, a "family" version for my kids and a version for my wife. Whatever you choose to include, I do hope that you give the gift of your journey to your family and others.

You have a story to tell. And, others, most importantly your family, will benefit immensely.

At the end of each season in this book, you will have a list of questions to reflect on your own journey. Check out the Seasons Journal if you need a detailed guide.

Contents

Preface: The Anchor

An object by means of which any construction floating in the water is attached to its position is called an anchor. An anchor provides stability, a settled, predictable position in a random flow of currents.

Beginning with a simple rock connected with rope to a boat, man has continued to engineer the anchor to include teeth and greater and greater mass. Today, the anchor is an integral piece of equipment that can secure the largest of vessels. In fact, these devices are so important that ships now have multiple, specialized anchors for use depending on the situation.

As long as there have been vessels on the water, man has recognized the need for an anchor. However, in man's personal journey through life, the recognition has not come so easily. Since creation, we have been drawn to live as if we do not need an anchor in life. We push, pull, fight, focus, meditate, and operate as if we control life's current. We believe our boat has been engineered to handle the water without an anchor.

At some point, in some way, every human will recognize the need for an anchor. It may happen alone in the quiet of a hospital room, with the only sound being the beep of the heart monitor. It may happen as life unravels before one's eyes. It may happen as one realizes the undeserved gifts they have received. But, make no mistake, the realization of the need for an anchor will come. We must have something to steady the ship.

And so it was with me. I needed an anchor in life—something that would bring me stability when the journey made no sense, when the water was shaky.

Like when I was left to die in the ghetto of Buenos Aires, Argentina. When I lost massive amounts of blood while I slept due to an overdose. When I was running from the police in Jakarta, Indonesia. When I saw five of my close friends die early in life. When I received a frantic call at 5:00 a.m. from my mom asking me to make the decision about resuscitating my dad. When I lost my father-in-law to a motorcycle wreck. When I watched my savings disappear as I sought to do good in the world. When I saw my brother, a dad of three beautiful young children, in the hospital with the nurses around him praying because there was nothing left that they could do. When I watched my business crumble with seemingly no way to control it. When I saw divorce wrecking the lives of husbands, wives, and kids who were close to me. When I lost six family members in three years. I desperately needed an anchor to cling to during these times.

Outside of my personal journey, I lived through rough times in our nation too, such as 9/11, when many lost their lives suddenly, unexpectedly before my very eyes. The world was at war, people were mad and confused, nothing made sense. And then there came the financial crisis of 2008, when many lost their fortunes overnight and took their own lives. People lost it all, and with it, they lost hope in the future. Both events rocked my world as well.

Fortunately, I discovered that priceless anchor for my soul. Looking back, it is very apparent that I would have never made it through this journey of life without an anchor. I needed something to steady my ship, as all these events happened suddenly, unexpectedly, with no advance warning. So many things were out of my control.

And, I suppose that my future will be the same. Many uncontrollables lie ahead for me. Many abrupt currents and changing tides are coming my way. However, with my anchor, I am now prepared to face the future. No matter the situation, the abrupt twist, the unforecasted storm, I can cling to my anchor to steady the ship.

The same will be true for you. Events are coming that will rock your world. Money, friends, faith, self-created gods, personal relationships, popularity, business, athletic prowess— nothing in this world will provide stability. You need an anchor that will steady the ship.

In a world of uncertainty, with many uncontrollable situations coming our way, I hope that you begin to discover the anchor that is there for you, the anchor of your soul.

We have this as a sure and steadfast anchor of the soul.

HEBREWS 6:19

Seasons of Life

I reflected on life one morning as I looked at a picture of an old college friend on Facebook. I had lost track of him, and apparently, life had not turned out as he'd planned. He was now about fifty years old and in a wheelchair, looking great, but his life had ended up in an unexpected place. The journey did not go as planned.

I looked at my own life. Like my friend, I certainly had not correctly forecasted the storms I'd encountered. I had not orchestrated the events that had transpired. My best developed plans never came to full fruition. My path was littered with tears of disappointment and confusion.

This left me to wonder, how much can we truly control? As I have walked the path of life, I have seen every journey imaginable, from those that led to stardom in the business world to those that had life end way too soon. I have seen the joys of victory and the damages of defeat. What is true for my college friend and true for me is true for all: life never turns out as exactly as planned. Behind every façade is a story.

As surely as the tide changes with the seasons and weather,

life changes. We change. We go through times of high tide and low, seasons that are calm and those that are tumultuous. Each season gradually dissipates into a fresh, new beginning. Before you know it, the years have flown by and there you stand looking back at your journey. That is why David Byrne's lyrics echo in my mind as I think about seasons: "How did I get here?" (For that reason, and because my friends and I used to imitate Byrne convulsing on stage in his live performance of the song.)

I believe it is a great thing to analyze your seasons. They help you know where you have been and, if you look closely, where you are going. After all, Solomon, the wise king of Israel, said there is nothing new under the sun (Ecc. 1:9). He also called life "meaningless" (12:8). Reflecting on his life, Solomon spoke of times in his life when he chased things in the world, saying these times were like chasing the wind (1:14).

If you look at the seasons of your life, you too will see that you were chasing things at different times, some meaningless, some meaningful. The meaningless times show the power of culture, the danger of folly, the inevitable picture of the fall of humanity. Oh, but the meaningful times. The times that are more than words can describe. The times that move the soul, like when you meet your wife or see your child for the first time. The meaningful times become etched in your mind, helping you remember the details of the season.

My story has all types of seasons—meaningful, meaningless, times that bring a tear to my eye or a smile to my face, times that make me fear, and times that make me want to convulse like David Byrne at the thought of the moment. The following is a sketch of my seasons that I wrote in April of 2018, reflecting on my life.

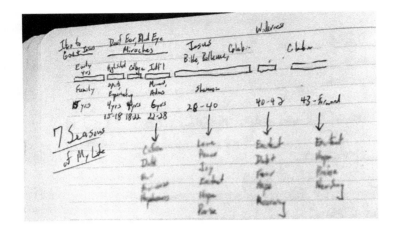

Purposely illegible, the drawing breaks my life down into seven different seasons, which I combine into five for this book. After many twists and turns as I followed my unique path, I discovered how I was built, why I think like I do, and how to find an anchor in rough water.

My desire for this story is that it would move you to likewise reflect on your own life. Don't waste the journey by floating through life without reflection. God sent you down your individual road for a reason. Find out what that is.

I hope through my story to also encourage you not to be afraid of the unknown, the uncontrollables that lie ahead in your path. Press in. Making it through the choppy water is where the joy lies, the learning is, and where the lessons that future generations need to hear reside.

So, I open the seasons of my life.

Season 1:
The Foundation

And the rain fell, and the floods came, and the winds blew and beat on that house, but it did not fall, because it had been founded on the rock.

MATTHEW 7:25 (ESV)

*F*ormative, family, fun. These are the words that describe my early years. I was blessed to grow up with an incredible family in a great community. Though I didn't always, I now know looking back the value of that.

My family was fun, safe, and secure. We had tight relationships, and I so enjoyed our time together. My dad was the leader, respected, feared, and loved. My mom loved my dad and always had my back. Divorce was never even a thought, and you didn't hear about it much in life. In fact, I can't think of one instance of divorce in our neighborhood.

With two brothers and a sister, competitiveness was instilled in me at a young age. There was always some type of game going on, whether it be inside hoops, outside hoops, or Wiffle Ball. I had to learn quickly how to control my emotions in the heat of the moment and how to win or else handle the trash talk.

There were things I could depend on, like family dinners. There were always six people around the table, and Mom always had casseroles, fresh vegetables, and sweet tea.

We routinely took family vacations, driving cross country like the Griswolds. At that time, in my community, there was no flying in airplanes. All the families drove. Summer always found us headed somewhere new and exciting, like Washington, D.C. or the beach or the mountains.

As most kids, I assumed everyone's life was similar to mine. At the time, in the '70s and '80s, the world was still a big place. The intricate details of the world were not known broadly. Computers, social media, and cell phones didn't exist. I couldn't look on my device at Bali, Indonesia to see the beautiful beaches. I didn't understand the poverty that existed in the Amazon jungle.

Outside of missing the next neighborhood Wiffle Ball game, I didn't have fears. War and hate weren't a part of my life. I didn't even know what prejudice or terrorism were at the time. A common fear among kids today is the fear of someone entering a movie theater with a gun and opening fire. That would have been a crazy thought to me. The world I knew was a safe place.

Comparisons weren't a part of my world either. As a kid, I don't remember labeling people as rich or poor or by what kind of house they lived in or by the car they drove or by the school they attended. None of this mattered. I was not in the middle of a "keep up with the Joneses" environment.

By today's standards, my neighborhood was abnormal. However, I suppose back then it was normal. The community was full of kids with the freedom to come and go as they pleased. We kids learned life together, formed a bond, a band of brothers and sisters.

The thought of life in rural Mississippi brings back special memories. I am who I am today because of it. The threads woven into my fabric during this season in large part composed the life that I live today.

We are all given threads in life, certain characteristics and traits that make us who we are. Some threads we are born with, and some we acquire along the way. This is not a process we control; we do not select the threads we are handed. We can, however, control the weaving. We must. We cannot sit by idly and allow the world to make of us whatever it chooses.

Throughout my early years, I had to cut some of the threads being woven into my life so that they would not be the predominant colors of my fabric. Others, however, I embraced, allowing them to be more defining.

Done well, our threads can be a lifeline, a guide. Our threads can help us manage the journey through life. The uncontrollables are inevitable, but the threads that display who we are can provide a point of reference, a perspective from which to view the world, a deep understanding of who we are and where we are going.

The Early Years

August 1969. Life for me began with Hurricane Camille bearing down on the coast of Mississippi. Maybe the hurricane was foreshadowing of a few seasons to come? With the hurricane warning in full effect, my mom grabbed her three kids, with me in the womb, and sprinted to Picayune, Mississippi for a few days to get out of the path. Smart mom, great move, as Camille became a Category 5 storm, the worst to ever make landfall.

My mom was strong. She knew how to take care of herself and her family and did so confidently. Nothing surprised her, and there was nothing she couldn't handle. Over the years she had developed a hardness, a toughness in her. Her home life had seen to that.

My mom grew up in Louisiana, in the middle of the state where there wasn't a lot going on. Her neighborhood's claim to fame was that Jerry Lee Lewis had graduated from her high school. From yearbooks, I saw that during her time my mom always made the homecoming court and was involved in her school.

After high school, Mom worked at the local paper mill. I picture her being the best employee at the mill, with eyes wide open to what was next in her career. I can't imagine her thinking that was her lot in life, especially since her dad was very entrepreneurial. She witnessed several of his businesses come and go through the years, all moderately successful.

She also witnessed something else. We all have demons in life, and her father's was alcohol. Although I was too young to pick up on it, he battled the bottle most of his life. This led to a challenging home environment for my mom, but she always felt loved and cared for by him.

Since her dad was an alcoholic for most of his life and her mom had a strong backbone, they didn't always gel as a couple. My grandmother never put up with my grandfather's behavior and seemed to constantly ride him. They were always arguing and bickering when I was around them. As a child, I remember asking them once not to argue so much. It is funny that I remember that comment. Conflict has always bothered me, and I believe the uncomfortable feeling that it gives me has roots here.

I don't want to understate the love that I felt from my grandparents, though. Some of my fondest memories from my early years are of visiting Louisiana with my brother and mom each summer to hang with my grandparents and cousins. During this time, my grandfather managed an apartment complex and had a pool maintenance business. I remember riding with him in his truck, visiting people's houses to clean their pools. I too remember the endless Wiffle Ball games in the apartment parking lot with my cousins. A home run went over a nearly eight-foot fence that we would have to scale to retrieve the ball in the middle of overgrown woods and brush.

Religion was important to my mom's family. Her one brother was a pastor of a small church in Louisiana, and I went to hear him preach as a child whenever I was in town. Although I can't recall a sermon, I do remember being proud that my family was leading the church. After church, we would gather at my uncle's house for a family lunch before going to the apartment complex for a swim.

Dad never made those annual trips to Louisiana with us. He always had to "work." I never understood why, but I now get it. I have fond memories of my grandfather, but apparently, drinking got the best of him most of his adult life, and for this reason my dad was never close to him. I never remember them together. I do remember them visiting us once, but it was very awkward with my dad.

My father grew up on a cotton farm. The old farm was a classic picture of life in rural Mississippi. All my relatives lived close to each other and leaned on each other for everything. The tough times were overshadowed by the joy of life done with extended family. Hard to imagine, but Dad called this time the "best of times."

Stories, stories, stories. Each story I heard from my Mississippi relatives provided insight into life in the rural state. Imagine no entertainment outside of what you created for yourself. No cell phones. No computers. No TV. No cars, or few cars. No technology.

The small town was a close-knit community. Everyone knew each other. Dad spent 100 percent of his time outdoors with his cousins and other close friends—a group of kids with no communication with the outside world. Life was what was in front of them, what they could see. That was the only reality they knew. It was truly a life that is foreign to our generations today.

One story that I remember took place when Dad's parents were away from home for a few hours. Dad was hanging outside with his cousins. As boys do, they began messing with each other, and one of them dared my dad to shoot one of the few cows that his family had, about one hundred yards away. As you can imagine, a cow was a big deal to a family in those days, in that town. And on the other end of the dare? My grandfather. My memories of my grandfather all involve respect and fear. He was serious, not a man to be messed with. So, this was a big dare.

Even still, knowing all the risks, Dad did what he would

always do in his life: he acted without fear. Too proud to back down from a dare, he went inside, grabbed his rifle, and shot. Being a great shot, down the old cow fell. An important source of food, gone.

Dad realized he was in hot water. Everyone deserted him, and he was left alone to figure out how to get out of the tough situation. He created a scenario in which the cow had succumbed to a heart attack. Dad told me about his fear, his panic, his crying, his lying, and his being found out. My grandmother believed the Bible verse that says, paraphrased, "spare the rod, spoil the child" (Prov. 13:24). Well, Mr. Rod met my dad's backside, and no more cows were shot. This is a great example of the antics created by a group of boys hanging out on a Mississippi country farm in the '40s.

On another occasion, as Dad and his group of friends were playing deep in the woods late at night, they stumbled upon a still. Moonshine was big business in the country. The moonshine was produced in barren areas of the woods, hidden from law enforcement. (However, I have a sneaking suspicion that the law enforcement may have been in the middle of the big business of moonshine. But you didn't hear that here!)

The only comparison to walking up to a still might be bumping into a drug dealer today. So at that moment, it was every child for himself. The boys knew enough to know that they were in hot water for the discovery. Ever see the scene in Forrest Gump where the boy runs everywhere, kicking up dust on gravel roads? That was Dad. He ran down the gravel roads to his house, then collapsed when he reached his family's long rock drive. When his dog, Bruno, jumped on him, he almost wet his pants. The boys never went in that area of the woods again. They now knew the boundary.

When Dad wasn't goofing around, he was working on the cotton farm. With no electricity, the sun was the alarm clock. It rose, and the family grabbed their burlap sacks and hit the fields to pick cotton alongside the farm help in the Mississippi heat. They worked until the sun went down. Dad used to tell stories of the times when he nearly passed out, guessing that they must have been instances of heat stroke. Never would you stop working, though, for fear of being perceived as not carrying your own weight for the family. Or worse, being perceived as weak. Kids today could never survive. Or, for that matter, neither could I.

I should mention, Dad wasn't paid for helping on the farm. When he wanted money of his own to spend, such as when the traveling movie tent came to town, he would visit his uncle. This uncle was one of the few family members with expendable income, given he owned the majority of the land in the area. He was also famous for building the first local cotton gin, having ordered the machine from a Sears Roebuck catalog—or at least that's the legend I never verified. Who knew a cotton gin could be built from parts in a Sears Roebuck catalog?

Dad would do whatever odd job his uncle needed him to do, and once the work was finished, he would hang around the house, never asking for money. After a long delay for effect, his uncle would walk out and give him a quarter. Dad would take the money and sprint to the movie tent, the closest thing to a theater in 1940s small-town Mississippi.

Church back in the day was apparently a hoot. In Dad's small country church, the preacher used to call people in the congregation to read a Bible verse or pray. Boy, that wouldn't fly today! Once, the preacher called a teenage kid to read, and the youngster was known to be illiterate. The young man was hesitating, fumbling through the verse as he attempted to make out the words. The preacher, thinking it was too dark, told the boy, "Step to the light so you can read." The young man, thinking the pastor was helping him read, proudly said, "Step to the light so you can read." The congregation broke the silence with laughter, and the boy sat down, shamed. Poor guy. Stories still circulate about his fumble.

Occasionally, revival preachers would come to town preaching fire and brimstone, all about the danger of going to hell. One night, an ugly storm rolled through with lightning and loud thunder, shaking the building. Dad thought the end had come and became scared to death thinking of hell. He talked about clinging to the hard, wooden bench where he was sitting. This picture epitomizes the old traveling tent revivals that used to be sprinkled around the South.

Inside my dad's home, however, faith was a more approachable subject. My grandfather was an avid reader and believer of the Bible. Under his guidance, my dad learned lessons like counting the farm and the work as a blessing from God and working as his family believed people were created to, "by the sweat of your brow" (Gen. 3:19). I never take for granted the faith of my grandfather and the lessons he taught Dad, as I would discover the value of faith and these lessons later in life.

So, how does a man like my father, poor and undereducated, make it out of rural Mississippi and life on a cotton farm? Most don't. If you go back today, you'll find that most of his old friends and family members still live in the area. Many still farm or work in small businesses in Jackson, Mississippi, the closest major city.

One would have expected Dad to do the same, carry on the tradition, work hard in the fields all his life. Not my dad. When he was about fifteen, sitting on the front porch with my grandfather after a sweltering day of cotton picking, he looked at him and said, "Dad, I love you, but there is more for me in this world. I am gone when I turn eighteen."

Dad had learned the value of hard work. The role of a father. The role of God. He had his foundation. And with it, he went the only direction he could go: he enlisted in the Air Force, his ticket out. Today, I believe that many have lost sight of the gift that the military can be for some. Sure, the military is a gift for the protection of our country. Where would our country be without it? Additionally, though, the military provides many individuals with a future. For my family, the military was an avenue to a different way of life. Dad's decision changed generations.

And his decision changed him, almost immediately. During his time in the military, Dad's eyes were opened to the world. He learned how a poor boy from Mississippi could mesh into doing life with those from other areas of the United States, and he learned about life through their eyes. In his new environment, he was a sponge—but he always acted like he was in the know.

My dad was enlisted in the Korean War, stationed in Alaska for most of the time. Pictures of his team are set against backdrops of beautiful lakes surrounded by mountains. He told me how he taught the others to fish, and in one picture, he is seen proudly hanging with his boys around a fish. His stance in this photograph is one I would see often—his chest puffed out, his gut sucked in, and an "I will kick your ass" look on his face.

After service, he enrolled at Southern Mississippi in Hattiesburg. A passionate Ole Miss Rebel until the day he died, how he ended up at the University of Southern Mississippi I am still not sure. He stayed in college for a couple of years, then heard about "high-paying" jobs being offered at South Central Bell in Jackson. He jumped at the opportunity.

Beginning at the bottom, on a crew hanging telephone lines, tirelessly climbing poles, he began learning the industry. This, for my father, was a glorious new start. Dad told a story about his first day on the job, when they pulled the truck over to take a coffee break. This was the craziest thing he had ever seen. First, why in the world did they need a break? Second, would they actually get paid for drinking coffee? Life was suddenly good. There was a different way to make money.

Dad noticed something else on this day too. He saw his coworkers relishing the coffee break and realized his point of difference. Nobody could outwork him. This was his edge.

Regarding the personal details of this time in my dad's life, I don't recall as much. One thing about our family's story is that there are always elements that are fuzzy, lacking detail. I have learned to stay in my lane and not ask a lot of questions. Some things in life are kept locked away in a closet never to be opened, because if you were to open that door, you would be bombarded with a different view of the world, maybe one that you would wish you never knew about.

I chose not to open the door to my Dad's first marriage. Apparently, he married when he was young and wild, with the union ending in his late twenties. I do not know about his first wife or their marriage. All that is relevant to me is that I have a brother and sister from this marriage. They are as much a brother and sister to me as my dad was my father. The terms *step* and *half* never made sense to me and are still not part of my vocabulary.

The story for me picks up when my dad was about thirty. One day, he went to repair a phone line at a paper mill in middle Louisiana. There he met a captivating young woman, my mother. He fixed the phone, flirted, and walked away with a new goal in life. He couldn't get this twenty-year-old off his mind. They began dating, sharing their backgrounds with each other. Dad shared his previous marriage and introduced the kids to Mom. Mom shared about her alcoholic father and introduced her parents to Dad. They both vowed "until death do us part," and so it was.

By this time, Dad had learned a great deal about the telephone system. He was the leader of major project after major project, and his leadership, work ethic, and "get it done" attitude earned him a promotion to district manager and then finally regional manager. Dad used to talk about leading all the individuals who had "engineering degrees out of big schools but no clue how to lead, work, or practically apply their knowledge." He was in his element at the phone company. He was fiercely committed to his work, and he genuinely cared about his people.

So, a handful of years after marrying my mom, as the hurricane was bearing down on the Mississippi Gulf Coast, our family sprinted for safety. Not my dad, though. The phone lines were critical. There was no internet, no cell phones. He had a job to do. Also, and perhaps the bigger reason, my dad still never wanted to be perceived as weak. He preferred people see him shoulders out, gut in, wearing that signature tough glance, not running away. For the company and for his image, Dad hung back on the coast to face Hurricane Camille head-on.

During the storm, he hunkered down with a few others on the ground floor of an office building. The winds during the worst of it roared at 150 miles per hour, the surge hit over 20 feet, and the coast was destroyed. Dad? He listened to the storm pass from underneath a table, and then he dove in, assessing, directing, owning the rebuilding of the telephone system. He walked away with the nickname Patton.

I was born a few months after the hurricane. We remained in the coastal area with Dad an integral part of rebuilding the only communication source. My parents often recalled those days, how life was good. For me, I don't remember them, but I wish I did.

I heard many stories of taking our boat out in the gulf to Cat Island, where we would fish, picnic, and hang out. Dad was quite the captain and fisherman, taking even the phone company executives out when they were in town. The execs used to visit frequently to go on these excursions with my dad. There were many stories of times we barely made it back to shore during storms, with one particular close call while I was asleep in the hull of the ship as a baby.

My mom used to recall the laid-back atmosphere of living on the coast. They would take the boat out to buy fresh oysters, shrimp, and crab directly from fisherman out on the water and host weekly neighborhood seafood boils for our tight-knit community. That community, that friend group, still has a special place in my mom's heart. Church, weekends, events, everything revolved around this group of people. They were like family. So much so that my mom never stopped missing them and the coast when we moved north.

Dad began getting calls for jobs that would promote him from a district manager to a regional manager when I was about four years old. Each required a move from the coast. The first offer would have made him manager over the Mississippi and Alabama areas and taken us to Jackson, very close to where my dad grew up.

We were very close to moving. I remember finding a farmhouse on the outskirts of Jackson with a good bit of acreage. I also recall Dad secretly "losing" the real estate agent and visiting the owner of the home by himself in an attempt to cut the agent fees out of the deal. Remember Dad's upbringing. He was tight with his money.

We went as far as touring a local private school. My closest brother wasn't fond of the school or the whole Jackson thing, though. So, for many reasons, mostly driven by the kids as I understand it, we remained on the coast.

Although Jackson didn't work out, the promotion opportunities would keep coming for my dad. Our family would be changing seasons soon, altering my personal journey in life.

The All-American City

L ife in the coastal city was coming to an end as more and
more opportunities came to Dad. The next viable option
for a promotion was in Tupelo, Mississippi, a small
town in the northern part of the state, about an hour and a
half south of Memphis. I don't recall the visit or the move, but
we made the jump in the late '70s when I was about four. My
oldest brother was fourteen, my sister was twelve, and my other
brother was eight.

Life didn't change much for me or my closest brother. We
were young, so moving at that point was nothing more than
changing houses to us. As little boys, we were able to just
jump into the new city. Immediately we found good friends in
the neighborhood.

However, for my older brother and sister, I know this move
was a lot more difficult. Although they finally found their
groove, it took a while. Like my parents, they loved life on the
coast, and now they found themselves in the middle of land-
locked North Mississippi. Listening to my older brother talk,
I gathered he mostly missed the freedom of riding motorcycles

with his friends around the coastal communities. He'd had tight friendships on the coast and now had to start over.

Tupelo, population thirty thousand, was an interesting town. It was a melting pot of sorts for the area. Few in the city were from Tupelo. Most people had migrated from other areas in the South for the growing furniture industry or one of the few manufacturing plants sprinkled around. Tupelo also was (and still is) considered the entertainment hub for many small towns around the area, believe it or not. It had thriving malls, theaters, and night life, making it the "big city" in North Mississippi to many country folks.

My family settled in a neighborhood surrounding a local elementary school. Our real estate agent pointed us to this neighborhood—a nice one, made up mostly of professionals spanning every industry. We moved a couple of times within the vicinity before settling in a home a few blocks from the school.

With little to no memory of the coast, my life began to take root here. Tupelo became my home, my love. And there was much to love in Tupelo. It was a fantastic place to grow up.

In my neighborhood, there were no less than twenty boys within a grade or two of me. My days were spent playing ball with them nonstop. Football, basketball, baseball, soccer—you name it, we tried it. When college sports changed seasons, our sports changed. We had makeshift fields, each with a name, each unique depending on the yard, spread across the neighborhood. When school was in session, we met in the afternoons to play ball at one of the fields. When summer came around, we played from dawn until dusk. We would go home for dinner and meet up at night for games of Kick the Can.

The fields were all special places to us. One family had a nice large side yard that was very flat, no trees. This was primarily our football field. The electrical wires overhead were perfect for field goals. A couple of other families lived across the street from each other, providing a great multi-yard field for Wiffle Ball. We always used a tennis ball at this field because of the distance required to hit a home run. Pop flies that would sometimes ricochet off one of the roofs were automatic outs. Our neighborhood elementary school had an awesome yard for all sports too, and everyone had a basketball court at their house, which saw a lot of use during basketball season.

Then there was the field in my backyard. My backyard field was a special place to me for a couple reasons. First, it took a monster shot to hit a home run over the trees. And second, you had to become skilled in catching balls falling out of trees, bouncing between limbs like a pinball game. The major obstacles at this field were the treasures that my boxer would leave. I remember cleaning the shoes of my best friend after he stepped in one of the treasures. As I cleaned, he was violently dry heaving off to the side. He had a very weak stomach—something we had a great deal of fun with over the years.

Always thinking about how to create the perfect sporting environment, my brother and I created a special ball, one that revolutionized Wiffle Ball (at least to us). We loosened the covers of baseballs, just enough to pull out the thread and hard core. We then took the cover and stuffed it full of Nerf balls before re-stitching the ball with thick wax thread. This ball mimicked a baseball—you could throw curves, sliders, knuckles—but it was perfect for our shorter field because you couldn't hit it too far. For a bat, we used a wooden baseball bat sawed in two at the top, with the handle left whole. The bat looked more like a paddle at the top.

I cannot imagine a better way to grow up than how I did. Everyone who grew up in our area probably shares the same sentiment. With no supervision, we boys ran the neighborhood. When we weren't playing ball, we were into something else, like catching crawfish in the creek that ran through the community. It was non-stop fun for a kid. Sadly, this is something few children get to experience today. Back then we didn't have any threats.

Peace is a blessing from God. This is a theme throughout the Old Testament. When there was peace in the land, there was great joy among the people. And so it was during my early years in our neighborhood. Our lives seemed to be full of peace, with so few cares in the world.

It is true, however, that when kids are left to roam the neighborhood, curiosity (and stupidity) takes over at some point. You learn about life. For example, I learned that there was no Santa Claus while catching crawdads in the creek. I learned that heaving filled water balloons at cars right as they crested the hill would cause near catastrophe, for the driver and all kids involved whose dads heard of it. Eventually I learned about Big Red chewing tobacco too. We boys would chomp it a few times each summer during our games. Half the kids would end up heads spinning, throwing up in the yard. We always tried it again, though. A dog returns to his vomit.

Through it all, our bond as kids became tighter and tighter. My friends' families were my families. I would maintain this closeness with a few of my friends through college, and although I rarely talk to them or see them now due to distance, I could have a conversation with them tomorrow and we would pick up right where we left off.

But what the Tupelo years did for my friends and me, they did exponentially more for my relationship with my brother nearest in age to me. While my oldest brother and sister were squarely in the middle of their teenage years, focused on friends and life, my brother and I spent countless hours in the backyard playing Wiffle Ball together, even without any friends.

On Sunday afternoons, I remember watching TWIB, *This Week in Baseball*, a popular show that reviewed the previous week of Major League Baseball. This show generated an energy in us that sent us running out to the backyard for a game of one-on-one Wiffle Ball. We had a major rivalry, complete with trash-talking, and most games would end in a brotherly fight. Since I was four years younger than him, I would end up on the short side of most of the battles, but I learned a lot of great lessons.

Lessons like how to hit a curve ball from a left hander. My brother was a lefty and could throw a wicked curve. Over time, that became the pitch that I waited on to swing. In my high school years, that never changed. I remember waiting on pitchers to throw curve balls, and I could easily take these pitches opposite field for a hit. However, fast balls were a different story. Once in high school, we faced a future pitcher for Mississippi State who had a 90-plus mile an hour fast ball. He never threw curves, and I struck out three times in one game, unable to lay off a high steamer. My brother couldn't throw 90 in the backyard, so I wasn't ready.

But seriously, the time with my brother taught me great lessons in life that I believe are missing today. I learned to control my emotions, as my brother would view this as a sign of weakness and capitalize on it. My laid-back approach to life is a direct reflection of my ability to control my emotions. This is a great skill in business.

Additionally, I was ingrained with competitiveness. These games with my brother taught me to be tough, to be focused, and, most importantly, to win. I am deeply competitive today when I become focused on something that can be won. I learned to fight for everything I got. There were no gimmes, nothing handed to me. This made me mentally strong. You must have that to compete in the world today, and I believe many kids grow up having all they want and miss this skill.

Despite the competitiveness, the fights, the rivalry, I became great friends with my brother. I looked up to him, and I would defend him at all costs. For example, all my cousins in Louisiana were once picking on him in the pool at my grandfather's house, and I remember standing up for him. Just the fact of my remembering this insignificant event when I was nine tells me how it impacted me. I remember standing up for him as he was fighting our next-door neighbor too. Again, an insignificant event remembered at a young age. It is interesting to note the random memories that are filed away that point to meaningful relationships in life.

This closeness with my brother would continue through most of my life. Whenever I would face struggles, the first person I would call would be my brother. I don't remember any wise advice, but I do remember the comfort I felt from knowing that my brother had my back and was there for me to lean on.

One of the main reasons I went to my brother first is because our dad was a disciplinarian with a capital D. Like his dad, "spare the rod, spoil the child" was a saying he lived by. We kids had a healthy fear of my father. He loved us and supported us deeply, but he also disciplined us. My brothers had great imitations of the way he would bite his tongue and pace as he became angry at our antics. I recall Dad making me go to our front yard to tear off a tree limb to bring inside to get a spanking. But, the worst was a spanking with his belt. This pain made you never want to be disobedient again—well, at least for a few minutes. But we all loved Dad dearly, and I so appreciate his discipline. The sons needed that discipline to keep us even halfway under control.

My mom, on the contrary, was the constant supporter, and we needed that too. She was a great offset to Dad. Mom was always with us, always seeing the good in her kids. All who knew her witnessed her defense of her kids. Don't get me wrong, she got some reality checks, but she demanded justice for her kids.

I remember in fifth grade when I did not do well enough on a test to make it into my school's honor program. The testing had not been communicated with the students' parents, so when Mom caught wind that I hadn't made the program, she stormed up to the school. She insisted that the test was broken and demanded that the school allow me to retake the test, because of course her son should be in the honors class. I saw the teachers converse in a circle outside the classroom after my mom's visit. I was allowed a retake of the test, same result. The gift of humility learned early.

I had an extremely close relationship with my mom, as I guess most sons do. During the tough times of my childhood, I would confide in her, the level-headed one. Dad was on the emotional side, often jumping to conclusions, battling a strong temper. Mom would guide me and work on Dad. Understand, she was not a pushover, but rather a very strong, logical thinker and very much the glue in our family. It took a strong woman to be married to my father. My parents were a great match.

Following after their parents, for whom church was a critical element to developing community, Mom and Dad continued the thread of religion in our family. (I say religion instead of faith, because there is a great difference.) In Tupelo, we became members of one of the largest Southern Baptist churches in the area. This church was full of boys my age, and I loved it. We were very involved with choir and mission trips in the summer with the youth group, and Dad tirelessly taught sixth grade Sunday school for many, many years. We used to have "lock-ins" at the church gym, where the entire youth group would spend the night. I remember all-night games of basketball and bowling (our church had a bowling alley of all things).

Church basketball became a central part of our lives. Dad coached various teams, and all three of his boys played in the city church league, a group of about ten churches. I have fond memories of teams, games, shots, and even injuries. Today, I can remember big shots that I made in different games—a testament to how much of an impact these plays had on me.

The topic of church brings me to another story. This one is a source of great internal debate in my life but a key element of my history. Like most churches at the time, our church had annual revivals. If you are not familiar with the old Southern revivals, they were brief periods of focused church time when preachers, normally from outside of the church, would speak to the congregation each night. Our revivals lasted a week and typically involved one preacher coming in to preach the entire week.

Mid-week during one revival, I was in the balcony with my friends, all of us around the age of twelve. At the end of the service, during the "invitation," a time when music is played and people are invited forward to "give their lives to Jesus," I responded, went forward saying that I believed in Jesus, and prayed with church leadership. After the service, I stood at the front of the church, and people lined up to offer hugs, handshakes, and congratulations. My family was there to support me too, save for my dad, who had to work. My mom said that she wished I would have waited until he could be there.

I remember the impact this event had on my life. Prior to this moment, I was unsure about where I would spend eternity, but after this moment, I felt peace, like a weight had been lifted from my shoulders. It was an emotional time, a real time to me. I can honestly say that I don't remember a dramatic change in my actions, though.

The process herein described, the "invitation" resulting in an individual's salvation, is typical in a Southern Baptist church. It is a subject of great debate among churches. This is not a book on theology, and as a rule I stay out of church and religion debates and use the Bible as my sole source of belief, but I will give you a simplistic, Mississippi viewpoint of the debate. Those not in favor of invitations believe them to be emotionally charged, sales-driven calls to people to say a prayer. Walking a church aisle, they say, is not in the Bible, and saying a prayer does not necessarily save an individual but can, in fact, be dangerous, potentially offering false assurance. Those in favor of the invitation process say that it is critical to accurately present the gospel at the end of every church service and give people the opportunity to respond to God by walking the aisle, processing, and praying with leadership. After all, we do not know when our last breath will be. I understand and agree with both sides of the argument, and honestly, I am fine with either.

A clear, absolute truth in the Bible is that belief in the Lord Jesus will save. That is the key. Belief is not simple head knowledge, as "even the demons believe" (Jas. 2:19), but heart knowledge by which you surrender your life to Christ. The Bible does not give limitations on when or where belief happens. It could be in a church service during an invitation. It could be walking down Beale Street at midnight in Memphis. The Bible does show examples of people coming to believe in church services, though. For example, in Acts 2 on the Day of Pentecost, after Peter preaches, three thousand people become believers and are saved. So, the core truth that belief in Jesus saves is enough for me, invitation or no invitation.

Outside of the debate, my response to the invitation was an important moment for me. This moment is a marker in my life that I look back to, remembering God's presence in my life. Was I saved at this moment? Did I become a believer in that church service? Honestly, I am not sure. It took me a long time to be okay with that, but I am now more than fine with that answer. I know God is sovereign, and I am secure in him.

After responding to the invitation, I was baptized, and this began my Christian life. Life continued as normal for me and my friends. We remained dedicated to ball, and more ball. Endless days were spent running the neighborhood, living a carefree life, staying out of trouble for the most part. Through fifth grade, our lives and minds had only known our immediate friends and the kids at our neighborhood school. Things were about to change, though.

In sixth grade, when seven elementary schools were consolidated for the first time into a new school, the kids from our neighborhood were suddenly mixed with other lives, other viewpoints, and other girls.

Previously, there was no reason to try to impress anyone. Everyone had grown up together, knew each other's families, and understood each other. Now, with this whole new set of kids, it was time to learn about other people, to position ourselves as leaders, and to experience new things. So, experience I did.

First up, sports. I remained focused on the big three: baseball, basketball, and football. To me, any leadership, popularity, and acceptance was based on sports. The kids from my neighborhood and I came to the consolidated school well prepared to play sports, so, along with the good athletes from other schools, we became leaders in the school. There was little peer pressure for us.

This athletic popularity led to interest from girls. Okay, that is a lie. The boys were the ones who all suddenly became very interested in the opposite sex. And we would do anything to let them know. I vividly remember passing notes on the playground, asking for boxes to be checked to indicate girls' rejection or acceptance of becoming the senders' girlfriends. Thinking back, this was a comical process. I remember having a note passed to a girl I had noticed on the playground. Unfortunately, I had the names mixed up and the note went to the wrong girl. I suddenly became the boyfriend of a girl I had never seen!

Through eighth grade, I remained occupied with clean, safe enjoyment of adolescence. I didn't have the opportunity to get into much trouble. My life was lived inside a Mississippi small-town bubble.

Then one day, when I was about fifteen, I went to a party in the neighborhood. Some other kids outside of the neighborhood came over with a bottle of Jack Daniels.

Innocence has a way of quietly leaving at a moment's notice.

Threads in the Foundational Season

Looking back, I realize the threads, both given and acquired, in the early years of my life made me who I am as a person today. As I mentioned at the beginning of the chapter, the threads can be positive and negative. The key is controlling the weave.

My fabric contained the beneficial threads of religion, work ethic, the "get it done" mentality, and a positive view of family. Some of my negative threads included alcoholism, the desire to be perceived as strong, and the ability to wear a façade and keep skeletons locked in a closet.

As you continue reading my journey, you will begin to see the impact of my foundational threads. The traits have always been there, through no choice of my own, but I would allow both the positive and negative traits to manifest themselves at different times. I would do little to control the weave.

Even today, my daily battle is to control my negative threads, because these will never go away. They are part of my tapestry, yes. However, I must stop them from surfacing so that their colors do not define who I am.

The positive threads given to me in adolescence, on the other hand, are my engine, propelling me in this world. I thank God for my foundational threads.

Reflect on your Season

For personal reflection, answer these questions about your early life.

- Describe your early home life, your parents, your earliest remembrance of life.

- Name the 5+ most impactful events that happened in your early years of life and write down the impact that each had.

- Who were the 5+ people that had the biggest impact on you early in life? Describe why they had such an impact.

- What core beliefs were developed?
    - View of people (stereotypes, ethnicity). Why did you have this belief?
    - View of the world (big/small, fears, travel). Why did you have this belief?
    - View of religion or church. Why did you have this belief?
    - View of God. Why did you have this belief?

- What impact did the area where you grew up have on your life? Think through the city, state, and area of the country.

- What storms came into your life and what was the impact of these storms?

- What threads were developed?

- What was your anchor during this season?

- Looking over this season, what are 3 pieces of advice you give your family, friends, the world.

Now, name this first season in your life. As an example, I

call season 1 in my life "The Foundation."

For a detailed format to record your journey, check out the Seasons Journal.

Season 2:
Deaf Ear, Blind Eye, and Miracles

For this people's heart has grown dull,
and with their ears they can barely hear,
and their eyes they have closed,
lest they should see with their eyes
and hear with their ears
and understand with their heart
and turn, and I would heal them.

—MATTHEW 13:15 (ESV)

I watched the young man mowing our back yard with a tear in my eye. A week earlier he had lost his dad, only fifty-one years old. His dad was a great man who cared for the lawns of half the people in my neighborhood. He worked with excellence. The neighborhood had a love and respect for him. A week earlier, I had talked to him about making sure our gate was closed after he finished cutting the grass. Now, I was talking to his son, telling him that I was sorry and praying for him and his family. An abrupt, unexpected end to his dad's life, and an unplanned twist in his.

The journey always has unexpected twists and turns. Any security we look for in this world cannot be found. Health, money, and the best of relationships will all let you down when you least expect it. Look around, examine humanity and you will see that this is an absolute truth. We live in an unstable world. That is why we need an anchor.

We lull ourselves into thinking we have complete control of life. We create a bubble, a seemingly indestructible defense against the potential storms in life. But the inevitable storm will come.

Reflecting on my foundational years, I realize the blessed life that I lived during that early season. However, in the moment, rarely do you take time to reflect on your seasons, your journey. This is especially true in your youth. I was oblivious to the blessings I had received early in life. I thought everyone was like me.

So, I entered season two eager to do life my way, chart my own course. Maybe it was because I was the youngest of four, or maybe it was because of the competitive nature instilled in me at a young age, but whatever the case, I was only concerned about the here and now and what I wanted to do in the moment. My mindset was not set on the long-term, where I wanted to go, what I wanted to be. I was never imagining what the future would be like. I was young and on top of the world. Implied in this thinking was that I was in complete control.

Sure, I believed in God, at least I thought I did, but my belief had never been challenged. After all, I lived in a bubble in Mississippi, oblivious to the outside world. This bubble created a misconception of control, a life in which dependence on God was not valued or needed.

Consequently, I shelved God and focused on myself. I entered this season focused on the things of this world, concerned about friends, sports, and being a social leader. Without my recognizing it, my life was molded into the culture of the time. Whatever was popular, whatever was fun, whatever made me edgy and gave me the appearance of fearlessness, I was in. There were few barriers, other than trying to fly under the radar of any authority, such as my parents.

On top of all the threads already woven into my fabric were added the threads of independence and leadership, both good qualities if controlled. I wanted independence, to do things my way. This fierce independence naturally created leadership. If my friends were afraid, I would go first as a leader. I became somewhat of a compass for those close to me.

The overarching thought was that I would live forever. The Bible describes this as the folly of youth (Prov. 22:15). As I reflect, in some instances, I wonder who this person was. If you only knew me in this season, you would be baffled at who I am today. That is the beauty of seasons. Just like a lifeless, dormant plant in the winter comes to a vibrant work of art in the spring, such is a life with the ebb and flow of seasons.

But, all of that deep thinking can wait. During this season, it was time to take on the world with no filters. Like a sailboat without a sail, left to be blown wherever the wind led, I was ready to follow life anywhere. I had no anchor, and I didn't feel I needed an anchor. Ironically, I loved the Talking Heads song, "Road to Nowhere."

Wandering

The simple life I enjoyed growing up a part of middle-class America in Mississippi continued into my teen years in the '80s. Life moved slow; life was good. Reagan was president, a presidential leader, and the economy was booming. The nation seemed unified, dominant too. There seemed little to fear in the world. Most importantly, America appeared stable, a blessed nation.

Once, when I was in Buenos Aires, Argentina, I spoke to a wealthy businessman about life in their country during the '80s. In the '80s, he explained, Argentina was a dangerous place to live and visit. Terrorism, in the form of bombs and kidnapping, had taken over the country. Imagine standing at a bus stop, reading the paper, waiting on your transportation, all the while wondering if someone in the group may have a bomb strapped to them. This is how the man I spoke with described daily life. The thought of terrorism was constantly on people's minds.

I remember his talking about how blessed the US was having never faced this fear. He then looked me deep in the eyes, penetrating my soul. He said, "The US will face it one day." It is amazing to me that a conversation like that from over twenty years ago stays ingrained in my mind. That was a powerful conversation. The man was a prophet.

The 1980s in America, though, found me at fifteen, at this party in the neighborhood, looking for a good time and craving popularity. There, a few boys, great guys I had gotten to know, invited me to the backyard. Some other guys were outside passing a bottle of Jack Daniel's around a circle, followed by a bottle of mouthwash. So, we each took a shot and washed our mouths out with mouthwash, hoping to mask the smell before we re-entered the party. Yes, we tried to wash the smell of alcohol away with more alcohol. The folly of youth.

I had never thought about alcohol before this. In fact, I had always vowed never to drink it, recognizing this behavior as a sin in the Southern Baptist church that caused nothing but issues in life. Maybe a legalistic belief versus a heart change?

I had also seen my brother come home once intoxicated. He stumbled down the stairs, and my dad woke up and helped him stumble back up the stairs (translated: threw him up the stairs). This didn't entirely take my parents by surprise, but the behavior was definitely not tolerated. I remember both my brother and I were thrust from our beds at about six o'clock the next morning to head over to one of the rental houses Dad owned and spend the day working on it. As we worked, my brother snuck around the side of the house a couple of times to throw up the previous night's ambition.

Nevertheless, in this moment at the party, without thinking, I jumped in. I wanted to be accepted by everyone. I was a people pleaser, and to me, this act put me on a different level of cool. My other friends from elementary school were great guys, I just needed to stand out from the pack, be recognized as a leader who would do anything. No fear. This was the makings of my mindset in the middle years.

Entering high school, I was the last sibling left living at home. My oldest brother had finished college and was working, and my sister had ended up in nursing and was now working at a physical therapist's office. As a lot of people in Tupelo do, both my brother and sister remained nearby throughout their schooling and working lives. Both married and had kids.

My closest brother had also just enrolled at Ole Miss, naturally. There had never been any other consideration. My brother and I practically grew up in the Grove, acquiring Dad's passion for the Rebels. We heard stories of the great Ole Miss and LSU games. I must have heard about the Billy Cannon punt return a thousand times.

I recall many Saturdays in the fall. We would leave Tupelo early in the morning, grab a bucket of spicy Kentucky Fried Chicken, and drive the hour and a half to Oxford. Tailgating was great fun, a carnival atmosphere. We mostly hung to ourselves, not tailgating with a group but finding an area to chill as a family. This upbringing drove my brother and me toward the definitive plan of attending Ole Miss after high school, and he was the first to take this path.

As most little brothers probably do, I looked up to my brother. I wanted to model my life after him. He was only four years older than me, so we were tight at that point in our lives. Always competitive, always arguing, but we had each other's back at the end of the day. To me, my brother was incredibly intelligent, cool, and great at sports. He seemed to always be a step up on everyone, the type of guy who walked into a room and owned it. He took that attitude to Ole Miss and was a social leader.

Life at Ole Miss was an eye-opener for him (and me). He lived in a trailer right off campus with a couple of friends. Yes, a trailer. The trailer was an idea dreamed up by my dad. Given his upbringing, always looking for ways to manage money more efficiently, he had the idea of buying a trailer and using this as a home for the next eight years for my brother and me. Great idea. I assume it was an incredible money saver for Dad. For my brother and I, there was a bit of a stigma associated with living in a trailer, but that stigma was quickly alleviated, as the trailer became infamous for many reasons, including the people who lived there and the parties that occurred within those tin walls.

Ole Miss has a reputation of being an old Southern

charm-type school, producing attorneys, doctors, and the like. My brother, accordingly, found himself rubbing elbows with old, deep money—the type of people who came from lavish lives of Mercedes and summer homes. But, my brother had something different that he'd picked up from his upbringing. He had threads that you obtain from more humble beginnings, often referred to as street smarts. He had a competitive fire, a will to win, and a personality and drive that would propel him to becoming a key piece of life at Ole Miss. My brother dove into the scene in Oxford and joined a fraternity, quickly making great friends with kids from all over the us.

Meanwhile, as I began to take on new experiences, my interests began to change. To this point, when it came to religion, I had leaned on what I considered obedience to God, what I was taught growing up by my church and family. This obedience included things like no cussing, respecting my elders (saying "yes ma'am" and "no ma'am"), praying at night before I went to bed, doing my best to be kind to others, and going to church on Sundays. As a child, this seemed like Christianity to me. You worked hard to stay in line with what the Bible teaches. Sure, you would mess up, but God was there to forgive.

I had always been told to read the Bible daily, have a "quiet time," but that didn't seem relevant to me. I never understood the need. Instead, I just began to drift slowly into the culture surrounding me, accepting truth as I saw it in society and open to whatever came my way. This type of living was relatively easy to keep in check before age fifteen, but about then, life hits you in the face.

This is true for all kids. At some point early in life, culture presses in and requires you to decide who you are and what you believe. If you wade into this water with no solid foundation of beliefs, you will be like a boat without a rudder, sailing to and fro wherever the wind leads. Make no mistake, though, you will make a decision. Either culture will mold you into believing the popular thoughts of the day or you will chart your own course.

Unfortunately, I was that boat without a rudder. I was into

popularity. So, my old thoughts were replaced by new life experiences and experiments. The God whom I was taught early in life didn't seem quite as demanding and big as I'd originally thought. Complete freedom was now at my disposal.

It was now my life to live, not my parents', my brother's, or my former self's. I had a journey to take, and my eyes were open to a different way of living with new things to try. Religion wasn't a focus area for me, but high school was.

The Golden Wave of Tupelo was a high school of a few thousand people, a slice of Americana. My friends were a diverse crew. I don't remember any prejudice at the school, as the Mississippi of those days continues to be portrayed. To me, everyone was the same, regardless of upbringing. There were no social differences among people because of the color of their skin, and I never understood why there should be. My dad, who grew up in the middle of extreme prejudice on the cotton farm in Mississippi, always shuffled us to and from basketball practice, taking care of all those who needed rides. He probably always fought the culture of prejudice that he experienced on the cotton farm. His view may have been tainted with his upbringing, but he protected mine.

Our high school was in the highest division in Mississippi in athletics, and Tupelo was known as a powerhouse in North Mississippi. Okay, powerhouse may be an overstatement, but that's how I remember it. I continued to be highly focused on sports, playing basketball, baseball, and football, until I finally focused on baseball my last couple of years. Interesting to note that baseball was my least favorite of the three, but my close friends played. I followed the pack. This group of friends that played baseball together did life together. We practiced ball every day and on weekends looked for things to get into.

After the night that I tried the Jack Daniel's, I watched my other friends begin to experiment more and more with drinking alcohol. In my view, they became part of the crowd, more mature, looked at differently by other kids, including the girls. My friends who were drinking were popular. Not that I wasn't; I was just on a different playing field.

So, like my friends, I adopted this lifestyle of casual drinking, making it as normal a part of my life as playing sports. My entrance into this scene emphasized my tendency to follow the crowd. The majority of people were moving this direction, so I jumped in the flow of the current. There was no logical reason why I shouldn't. There was church and what I was told the Bible said, but as I have alluded to, culture was a much stronger influence than what I was hearing (or not hearing) on Sunday morning. Culture was real, tangible, fun.

My closest circle of friends was made up of about seven or eight people. I'm not sure how we all ended up being close friends, but it was a combination of church, sports, and just being introduced at school. We did everything together, and these guys knew more about me and who I was than anyone else during those years. We were learning life together—learning how to fit in, what was important and not, what our worldviews would be, and where to spend our time.

It is interesting how friendships blossom and mature. You know when you have real, close friends. I can point to one guy from high school whom I would consider a "forever friend." Not to say that I couldn't immediately pick up with the others in a conversation and never miss a beat, but I did have one friendship that stood the test of time. We knew each other from early on in the neighborhood. His house was my second home growing up. We walked through some extremely difficult family situations together, such as the death of his brother, and we walked through many joys together, like his hitting a half court buzzer beater in fourth grade to win a game. I remember that shot and the ensuing madness like it was yesterday.

I also find it interesting, as I look at that circle of friends, the different journeys that we all took. All of us went to college in Mississippi, either junior college or a major university. A high percentage of the friends ended up living around the area, mostly in business, some becoming leaders in the community. Of those who left, several moved to the "big city" of Memphis and several eventually moved back to the area. And, as with most high school circles I guess, a couple of boys in our group passed away in their twenties. Actually, a pretty high percentage ended up having their lives end way too soon. (One such person was the leader of the Jack Daniel's incident, who, I was told, was found dead on the streets in a major city in the Southeast. The story was that he ended up homeless, addicted to crystal meth.) It would have been hard to imagine that this could happen when we were living the carefree days of high school.

Tupelo high schoolers made plans throughout the week for where we would meet up on Friday night for the next party. The majority of the time, we met up behind the old drive-in movie theater, a site that had not been in operation for many, many years. We built a bonfire, played music, mingled, and drank. As I remember it, the majority of the high school would be at these parties. It was a movement that everyone was participating in, if you were anyone.

The parties went well into the night, moving to someone's house if parents were away. Occasionally, the police would break up the party, sending everyone scurrying their separate ways. I don't ever recall the police being seriously upset with anyone or jail time ramifications. There was, however, the time one of my good friends was running through a field from the police and fell into a fifty-foot well, wedged in a U shape. He ended up fine but came away with the story of a lifetime, which made headlines in the paper.

Once, I threw the party at my house. As I mentioned, if someone's parents were headed out of town, the news was always circulated around the high school and a party ensued. When my parents took a weekend trip, the opportunity was too good to pass up. So, party we did. I remember people at my house I didn't even know. At one point, I had to ask people in the bathroom to "please smoke the joint outside."

I woke up early the next morning and cleaned until I was blue in the face. My only concern of getting caught was that my house smelled like smoke. My parents arrived home and were completely oblivious. They asked how the weekend went, and I answered that it was "pretty boring." However, much to my dismay, my mom called me in the kitchen with a question: "How did a Bud Light beer label end up stuck in the back of the oven?" Really? Thanks, friends!

Early in high school, these parties gave me the opportunity to befriend older kids, those further along in their journeys than me. With these relationships, I took further steps into my own journey, experimenting with smoking and marijuana. I liked to be perceived as the individual who lived on the edge. Plus, I enjoyed it. I was typically the first one in my close friend group to experiment with something new and bring others with me.

My best memories from this time in my life, however, are not those of partying, though they are plentiful. My best memories are the simple stories of life in high school in Mississippi. For example, the memory of my best shining moment in baseball. First inning, first game of my senior year, I was the lead-off batter facing a pitcher who would end up throwing at Ole Miss. First pitch of the game, I homered over the left center fence. Always one to have "warning track power," as my coach used to joke, I almost knocked his arm out of socket rounding third base with my high five.

I also remember, in the first month I had my driver's license, after playing pickup basketball with my friends, I was driving home when a drunk driver rear-ended me. My dad arrived at the scene prior to the police and, let's just say, let the man know that he didn't appreciate his drinking and driving. Luckily for the man, the police arrived and took him to jail.

Many stories exist of these high school days, of playing sports, experimenting with new things in life, and general youthful exuberance. When I compare the stories of my youth in Tupelo to the stories of my dad's youth from the farm, I see the stark contrast of the two generations. His pursuit of "better things" in life away from the cotton farm changed my journey, making my stories of youth radically different than his. My stories show hints of budding materialism, mainstream culture influence, and entitlement. They each individually reflect the trappings of a comfortable life in a Mississippi bubble. Indeed, Tupelo High School was an incredible place to grow up. "Glory days, they'll pass you by, glory days, enough to make a young man cry, glory days" (sing along).

And then, I was set to be a Rebel. The trailer was set up at Ole Miss, waiting for me, I knew the campus well, and I was known in my brother's fraternity. The road had been paved for me. My family was prepared and eager to celebrate the start of my Ole Miss career. However, there was a dark day coming on the horizon for our family.

The Road Much Traveled

One can choose a couple of different paths in college. Choose well, because your life journey will be greatly impacted by this decision. Even more important is the impact you will have on others by this choice.

The first path is counter-cultural, the way of the minority. I call it the road less traveled. To take this route, you must have strong foundational faith and know who you are, what you are about, and where you want to go. On this path, an individual follows their passions and heart, strategically, to a place or area of study, choosing a university that positions them for the future. The people on this journey have their heads on straight and have the potential to positively impact others during college. They go to school to learn, to position themselves for the future, to lay the foundation for their lives.

Imagine four years spent positioning yourself for the future and positively impacting others. What an awesome opportunity for kids. Make no mistake, the connections and positive impact you have on others in college will change generations.

The alternate path is directly opposite the first path. On the road much traveled, individuals jump in the current and allow the flow of the culture, to carry them where it may. Honestly, this is a very easy route to take, requiring no faith and only a people-pleasing, popularity-driven attitude. The pursuit of popularity, of fitting in with the crowd, overrides long-term, strategic thinking about any area of study or the future. Social life is of prime importance, and no implications are considered. A key marking on this path is the negative impact you will have on your own life and, inevitably, those around you. This impact will not show up immediately, but rest assured, generations will be impacted. There are consequences.

As I write this section, I think about how social media naturally pushes our kids to the road much traveled. Social media is all about following culture, building a fake life, keeping up the perception that you are a rock star. This is a dangerous route.

But, even before social media, reflecting on my path, I, along with many others, chose the road much traveled. I never thought strategically about my future or what I wanted my life to look like. As I thought about college, I was more interested in where my close friends were going. At the time, to me, these relationships were more important than the university. And wouldn't you know, most of my friends were going to Mississippi State, not our family's beloved Ole Miss. Additionally, I had become good friends with several current Mississippi State students.

So, for me, the decision was easy. I would become a Bulldog at Mississippi State. I made the announcement to my family, and there was turmoil.

To understand why I say "turmoil," you must understand Southeastern Conference rivalries. They run deep—too deep for one to understand if they are not from those parts. True, there are many similarities between Ole Miss and Mississippi State, similarities which I am sure hold true at any campus in the SEC. Football is king, the Greek system is the source of the social scene, and education is secondary to campus life. Apart from those few points, though, the two universities are radically different. During the time I was attending, one school was known as an elitist school and the other was a state school. Ole

Miss, the school known for its Southern charm, drew students from all over the nation. Mississippi State drew students mostly from Mississippi and the Southeast. Ole Miss was known as a heavy party school, while Mississippi State was a bit quieter.

Around Thanksgiving, the whole nation stops for turkey. Not in Mississippi. At Thanksgiving, the state stops for the Mississippi State and Ole Miss football game. In fact, to maintain peace with my brothers, I don't watch that game with my family. We literally almost came to blows once when we watched a game together. There is deep, bad blood between the universities.

So, naturally, my brothers were destroyed at my news. They could not agree with my decision and tried to convince me not to go to the "cow college." It would be boring, they said, a terrible place to go to school. They told me that I could not treat our family that way. We had too much heritage; we were Ole Miss Rebels. And I really was. I mean, I loved the Rebels. I had scrapbooks of old articles about Ole Miss football. The Grove was an awesome place that I cherished.

However, my mind was made up. I was not going to choose my college based on something as shallow as my family heritage. I was going to Mississippi State to get a good education. I laugh as I write that. I was going to Mississippi State because most of my best friends decided to go there. This was a collective decision made by all of us. We would get to hang out for four years, and the trailer would be left in Oxford where it belonged.

The trailer. Who can forget the trailer? Dad's financial savings plan. (Actually, as I currently stare college expenses in the face, I realize the trailer was an innovative, genius plan. In fact, maybe this is foreshadowing for my kids!) That trailer had developed a history by now. The year after my brother graduated from Ole Miss, not wanting to leave Oxford, he hung around waiting tables, living the vibrant college scene. He moved into a house with a few friends and rented the trailer to some people he knew. Apparently, the trailer turned into quite the narcotic distribution hub. The police ended up busting the trailer and, in their search for drugs, completely destroying the place. I never knew exactly what happened—one of the many skeletons that the family keeps locked up in the closet.

Destroyed or not, Dad was never one to have his plans relinquished without a fight. After all, the trailer was a paid-for asset. So, he refurbished it and had it moved to a place right off campus in Starkville, Mississippi. The trailer would be my home for the next four years.

I remember my parents taking me to the trailer when I started school. Other dads apparently had the same financial savings plan as mine, because there were other college students living all around the yard. This plan is probably a Mississippi thing. In fact, I am sure it is a Mississippi thing. I must say, though, the feeling of independence in that tin building was pretty awesome. It was my own place, right by campus. I entered college with a new kind of freedom and uncontainable excitement.

My college years actually started the summer before the first semester of classes, when I began attending the fraternity rush parties. These parties took me to greyhound races in Alabama, the Gulf Coast, and various locations around Mississippi. My Tupelo crowd and I began to have our eyes opened to Greek life, and we loved it. At the parties, Tupelo graduates who had been in fraternities at Mississippi State would take us under their wings and introduce us to all the members of the fraternity. The parties laid the recruiting groundwork for us to become members. They paved the way for my social life in college. Rush week was next.

Rush week kicked off the new school year by having incoming freshmen desiring to enter the Greek world attend a week of meetings at each fraternity. My eyes were opened to a broad range of people and life on campus during this week. Of the fraternities I met with, one was known to have a lot of college athletes. I remember hanging out with a few of the players on the MSU baseball team. Cool guys. A bit conceited as I remember, but they left an impression. Another fraternity had a lot of people from different areas in Mississippi. I knew no one at this house, no one from Tupelo was there, but I did find myself drawn to them.

I was never closed-minded to any of the fraternities. In fact, I would end up frequently hanging out at other houses with other frat members. To me, fraternities were simply places to enter the social scene and make new friends. Some people were almost cultish with their fraternities. Not me. I was in it for the social scene, plain and simple, no matter the Greek letters.

After the crazy week of meeting all the fraternities, going from house to house, the selection process commenced. Each club conducted a meeting and selected those who would receive bids to their fraternity or sorority. The meetings were similar to a scene in the movie *Animal House*. Pictures of individuals were held up, and the room cheered or booed or, as in the movie, threw stuff at the screen. Okay, it wasn't quite as dramatic as the movie, but close. Once the club determined the people who would get the cherished bids, they gave the selections to the people running the event. These meetings happened among the approximately ten fraternities and ten sororities on campus. And then, bid day arrived.

On bid day, all the students who went through rush went to Humphrey Coliseum, the basketball arena. Sitting in chairs on the basketball court, we, numbering over five thousand freshmen, were each given a unique envelope. Members of the different houses circled the court holding banners representing their respective fraternities or sororities. Each group was chanting, screaming that they were number one.

Upon receiving the envelope, each student read his or her bids. Some had three bids, some had five, but I think everyone was guaranteed at least one somehow. In today's "everyone is a winner" world, this probably seems like a cruel selection process. In fact, I bet it has changed. However, it was great fun for me. I wasn't thinking of others. I had to protect my social status in college. I was only concerned about receiving the one bid I wanted. And I did.

What happened next was complete chaos. The leader of the meeting shouted, "Go!" and each incoming freshman seated across the floor made a mad dash to the section in the bleachers housing the fraternity or sorority of their choice. After I reached the section for my fraternity, we were whisked out of the gym, loaded onto a bus full of testosterone and wild-eyed college kids, and taken to a massive celebration full of kegs, funnels, you name it. After a couple of hours of celebration, we rode the bus back to the fraternity house, lined up, took a pledge to become members of the fraternity, and received our pledge pins. Then, let the party begin.

The social scene of college was a whole new world to me, and, as always, I dove in headfirst, looking to lead the pack. My days were spent playing pickup basketball and flag football and hitting the social scene. Heavy drinking and all-night parties ensued.

Education was important to me, but only to "make my grades" enough to keep my parents happy and keep me in school. I still remember entering my first freshman class with about five hundred people in an auditorium. What a change from high school. They would have no idea if I was in class. Awesome, I thought, but in reality a recipe for disaster for a boy always looking for the next party.

This type of accountability, or lack thereof, spelled early exit from Mississippi State for many. But, my dad was my accountability. I always made sure I carried a 3.0 grade point average, and I was responsible enough to study when needed. I spent extra time in the library as required, and, just like today, I would rise extremely early to cram for tests, as I learned best in the early morning hours. I was serious enough about college to make sure I didn't have an early exit, but that was the extent of my ambition.

Freshman year, the school work was a breeze. I didn't need to listen much in class. I remember sitting in one of those large classes once, opening the paper and full spread reading the sports column. I was completely oblivious to the world around me. The lecturer stopped the class and said, "You, in the red shirt, reading the paper. Please put that down or you will leave this class." I didn't hear the lecturer, as I was engrossed in the news. I kept reading until those close by slapped me on the arm. I put the paper down, looked up, and the class erupted in laughter. That must have left a mark on my brain, because I remember it vividly.

A few months later in this same class, after an all-nighter, one of my friends entered late, still hazy from the night before. The only open seats were at the front of the large auditorium, so, as the teacher was talking, he made his way down the aisle. With each step, a wave of laughter spread, following his walk. When he sat down, he looked around, wondering what was going on. Someone leaned over and told him that his three-button golf shirt was on backwards. He was indeed a bit foggy that morning.

Outside of the classroom, life was happening, moving fast. Starkville, Mississippi was a college town, plain and simple. A town of about twenty thousand people, the university was the lifeblood, the existence of the community. Hold your judgment, because it was a great place to experience life. Starkville was all I knew, so the diversity of students, the different thoughts, and the different ways of doing life were exciting to witness. From the sausage on a stick and great bar-b-que at Lil' Dooey's to the magnitude of SEC sports to great home cooking at the square, Starkville was an incredible experience for me. My only regret is that I lived most of the four years in a college haze. The cloud that began in my high school years continued to grow at a rapid pace.

The innocence of that fifteen-year-old kid from Tupelo who was into sports was no longer around. I had allowed the current to sweep me away. I was a different person, continuing to experience new things. This happens to many a young child. Before they know it, they become radically different people, throwing their weak foundational beliefs behind.

Throughout college, people from Tupelo would remain my friends, but my best friends were people from all over the state. My new friends in college tackled life at the same rate of speed I did. These kids were looking for a great college experience via a wild social life, the party scene. That is how we measured ourselves.

While days were spent playing pickup basketball at a few different frat houses or the tin gym on campus, nights were spent getting to know each other at the Landing, the local hangout. Essentially, the Landing, which I heard has since burnt down, was a gigantic metal building, half pool tables, half bar tables. This was one of the local watering holes where we spent a lot of time.

As fraternity pledges, we hung close, knitted together in our love for Mississippi State, freedom and independence, sports, and binge drinking. The latter was done hard and often. Looking back, it seems this was how we unintentionally made a name for ourselves. Our circle of friends quickly became known as the go-to people if you were headed out on the town or looking for a good time. We all very much had the try-anything attitude—emphasis on *anything*. We were influencing each other with every step we took.

Similar to at Ole Miss, the Starkville version of the trailer became famous for parties. We had pre-game parties before heading to the Landing or another local club that had perpetual live music. And after the evening, most of the time, we ended up back at the trailer, drinking or smoking pot, usually both. The trailer almost seemed like a pit stop for people looking to hang out. Someone was always stopping by, whether between classes or on their way to an evening full of partying. When people came by, I always jumped into the party, open to wherever we were going and whatever we were doing.

One night, midway through my freshman year, I was introduced to a new way of having a good time. Up to this point, I never really looked for new highs, new drugs; marijuana was fine for me. Also, truth be told, I never liked getting high. The drug makes you extremely laid-back and lethargic and puts your mind in a fog, and personally, it made me eat a large cheese pizza from Domino's every single time. So I would get high with everyone, but it wasn't something I craved or looked forward to doing. On this night, however, I was introduced to a drug with an opposite effect, a pill called ecstasy.

As I remember it, a few of the older guys in the fraternity invited me and another friend for a night of partying. It was an off night, a Sunday night, so not a lot of people were going out. We were going to take ecstasy at the frat house and then hit one of the local venues. Ecstasy was on-trend on college campuses, at least in Mississippi. I vividly remember being asked if I had ever done the drug, and I proudly responded, "Many times." And just that casually, that night began my journey of narcotic experimentation and finally abuse. I was never addicted but always ready to have a party.

Word got out around my friends about the ecstasy-filled evening, and they were curious. So, I did what any good leader would do. I talked it up, and we had our own ecstasy experience.

As we finished our first semester in college, those of us who made our grades were initiated into the fraternity. So long as we made it through "hell week," we were no longer pledges. No more cleaning up after parties, saving seats at football games, or any other type of servant work for the fraternity. We were ready. One more week. Nothing to it. Why was it called "hell week" anyway? I would soon find out.

Hell week was, well, a week full of sleep deprivation, crazy antics, yelling and screaming, getting ridiculed by the members, and complete embarrassment. The practice of "hazing" has settled down over the years, but back in the day, hazing was the name of the game. To kick off the week, the fifty pledges were each broken into groups of two or three, housed in separate rooms of the house. We stayed up forty-eight solid hours with the task of memorizing twelve principles of the week. As I understand it, these twelve principles were put together by a sadistic individual, created so that they were impossible to memorize. Members would enter each room, berating the pledges for not knowing the "rules." You heard the screaming, crying, and wailing throughout the house. Evenings brought blindfolded trips to the woods, where we would sprint, remaining blindfolded, while being asked to jump ditches, dodge trees, and trust our leaders. We were not allowed to talk to other pledges. That was a big no.

In one experience, each pledge was pulled out of his room one by one and asked to put on a blindfold and place his hand on a member's shoulder. The member would say, "Are you ready?" At the sound of yes, they would sprint through pitch black halls of the frat house, with members lined up pushing the pledge back and forth. The run would continue up the stairs until you entered a small room, where the blindfold was removed. You found yourself staring in a mirror, sweating, scared, heart racing as someone behind you read the poem "Don't Quit." You know, the one that goes, "When things go wrong as they sometimes will. When the path you are trudging seems all uphill. Rest if you must, but don't quit." Yada, yada, yada. Thanks for the encouragement. Some did try to quit, literally running out of the fraternity house during the week. The members always talked them off the ledge and into staying, though.

So, initiation came and went, and we settled into college life. SEC football was a main focus of college life, a ritual in the South. It truly gets in your blood, regardless of what SEC school you attend. As the modern commercial says, "It just means more."[1] Crazy, but it does. Mississippi State football was just beginning to gain momentum, and our crew would load up to travel to many games.

I recall being in Hattiesburg watching Mississippi State take on one of our in-state rivals, Southern Mississippi. MSU won in overtime over a future NFL quarterback. That night was wild. I remember a security guard starting to walk up the middle of the MSU student section, only to walk back down after someone hurled an empty beer can at him.

Loudest stadium I have ever been to? Without a doubt, Death Valley at LSU for a night game. Along with the LSU fans, we arrived at the stadium early and stayed late. We joined in the party until the game was over, with MSU losing by about forty. Hey, we were only there for the party, though, so all was well.

After the games followed all-night parties at the frat houses. I would hop from house to house hearing local college bands play. None of these bands ever made it big, but they were big in our book.

When it wasn't football season, there was SEC basketball and baseball, two sports in which MSU had success while I was there. In basketball, student seating was first come, first serve. Our crew was always the first in line to enter the stadium, and our fraternity took over a small set of bleachers courtside below the student section. Everyone would hide their pint, and we enjoyed awesome basketball.

Who can forget Hank Flick, State's announcer, settling the crowd in with his signature "For an evening of basketball, Mississippi State style." The crowd would say it along with Flick. We saw players like Shaq, Chris Jackson, and Todd Day roll through Starkville. I remember Todd Day grabbing a jump ball, taking a few dribbles, drilling a three-pointer, then having a word with the student section. Beautiful.

In baseball, MSU was always a powerhouse (at least in my mind, kind of like my high school baseball team). Like the sport, the baseball events were laid-back, involving hanging out in Left Field Lounge. Fraternities or other groups of people would lease areas in left field and construct makeshift bleachers on top of giant open-bed trailers. Everyone would grill, drink cold beer, and hang out for the afternoon. I don't remember much about any individual games, as gatherings at Left Field Lounge were purely social events, a tradition at Mississippi State. They were a great way to kick off a Saturday party.

My personal participation in sports continued to include endless—and I mean *endless*—hours of pickup basketball. A group of my friends and I won the Schick 3-on-3 tourney at Mississippi State and advanced to the regionals at Arkansas State. Our fraternity gave us travel expenses, and we hit the road to Jonesboro. But, the unfortunate thing was that we had to travel through Memphis to get to Jonesboro. We ended up hanging out with my brother in Memphis, most notably at the greyhound races in West Memphis. "Kid Tango," a nickname given to one of my friends that evening, won a big race. We did play pickup basketball in Memphis that weekend but never made it to Jonesboro. No one at MSU would have known, except that a referee from school went to Arkansas State to help call the 3-on-3 games. He came back asking why we never made it. We quickly quieted him down, and the discovery was never widespread.

In addition to pickup basketball, we were knee-deep in flag football. We won the campus championship every year I was in school, which had us competing in the flag football national championship tourney annually in New Orleans around New Year's. Imagine that each year. Eleven of my fraternity brothers and I spending New Year's playing flag football at the University of New Orleans. Great fun, tons of memories from those trips.

We had a great offense, spreading three quarterbacks across the field behind the line of scrimmage. No other school ran this unique offense, and it was deadly (if I do say so myself). At the national tournament, the good teams had offensive machines. There was a lot of flipping the ball back and forth and quick movements, and there were no plays—more closely resembling sandlot football. To win, you had to stop these offensives a few times and score every time you touched the ball. Little margin for error existed.

Never losing a game at Mississippi State, we made it out of pool play at the national tournament every year and to the final eight twice. However, our last year, we made it to the final four, one game away from the championship game, which was played at the Sugar Bowl in the Superdome during halftime. Down by about four, something like 56 to 52, we had the ball on their ten-yard line, about to score on the last play of the game. The quarterback on the right threw a pass to me, the quarterback on the left, on the final play. I was to catch it, then hit our best receiver on a slant for a touchdown. The cross-field pass was high and caught by the wind, and I ended up in a dead sprint backwards to retrieve the ball, never getting to it. The ball fell to the ground. Game over. No Superdome. So close. I can still feel the wind in my face that I felt as I sprinted to the ball. Nevertheless, we were in New Orleans at New Year's, so the party commenced as expected soon after the game.

The parties that circled the sports became wilder and wilder, taking my friends and me deeper with drugs. After trying ecstasy the first night, I progressed to regular use. We would all gather, about five to ten of us depending on the evening, and take the pill at the same time to enjoy the buzz together. I remember sitting around a table waiting until the seven o'clock hour before we all toasted and swallowed the pill with our beer. Then, it was on to a bar that had live music, to which we would dance the night away—the main effect of the drug. For some reason, with ecstasy in your system you feel like Michael Jackson on the dance floor. Must have been quite a sight with us all out on the floor flailing around like we had dance moves. Thank God cell phones had not yet been created.

At twenty-five dollars a pill, ecstasy made for an expensive night, so the cost kept our use a bit under control. There was, however, LSD, or "acid" as we called it, a cheaper alternative. With LSD, consistently I would have what is called a "bad trip." A "bad trip," as defined by me, is when you become anxious, have irrational fears, and generally lose your right mind under the influence. I remember hallucinating that everyone in the bar was laughing at me. This anxiousness was led by my friends, who were also tripping, making fun of me because they knew my tendency to be freaked out by acid. So, given the occurrence of "bad trips," LSD was not my preferred drug of choice, but most of my friends liked it, so I dove in.

Then, somewhere around my junior year, I was introduced to a drug that would almost end my life: cocaine. Although very expensive, "coke" provided an immediate high, a heart rate increase that sent one zooming into the night. We would gather at the trailer, line up the powder, and snort before going out. Quick, sudden rushes. The big drawback was coming down. Deep, depression-type feelings would fall upon people after a night of using the drug. I remember coming in the trailer and seeing my roommate crying one night about some things going on in his life.

Honestly, as I work through this era of my life, it is troubling. I don't know who this person was. Most troubling is the fact that I was an extremely negative influence on so many. As

I recall the memories, I have trouble getting the words out. It isn't easy for me to revisit those times. But to understand where I am today, I must understand where I have been. My journey is sweet when I remember where I have been, because, as you will come to see, this life is evidence of a forgiving and patient God.

Through this time in college, there wasn't much to my religion. I never went to the Baptist Student Union, as that place lacked anything close to a good time, and I never went to a church, knowing it would just condemn my actions and potentially make me feel guilty. I remember checking the box by consistently praying a ritualistic prayer that included the words, "Please forgive me for smoking and drinking." But that just shows my definition of religion was more of a list of dos and don'ts, not a true change in my heart to the extent that I fell in love with God. Religion and church would stop my good times, and I didn't want to wade in those waters.

In between the sports and partying, I did pursue many different girls. At that point in my life, females were secondary, though, to my friends and college life in general. I may have seriously pursued a couple of girls, but I do not know why they would have been interested in me. I was a dangerous, wild influence in their lives.

So, I think you get the picture of my college life—SEC sports, intramural sports, fraternities, and drinking and drugs. These were carefree times. College was a time of meeting new friends, experimentation, and learning to live on my own. I would take nothing for my time in college, as I have great memories.

However, I could have been so much more productive and efficient. In fact, if I could do it over again, with my head on my shoulders, I would be sure to be a positive influence on many. I would live my faith and draw others to the God I met at age twelve and the God I would know much more intimately later in life. Instead, I was the opposite, an influence toward what I considered the "normal college life."

Deep down, I think I knew even during college that at some point I would need to fall in line, but college was not the time. I respected those in the church a lot, but for me, the rules and regulations of practicing religion were not appealing and seemed to amount to an antiquated way of living. Religion equaled to conforming to legalistic rituals. One thing is for sure: I am not a conformer, never have been. The nonconforming thread was given to everyone in my family, and that seed was definitely planted in me. I didn't conform or pay attention to rules. I fought them. And I still do today. I am not saying this is the way to live; I'm just acknowledging my Mississippi thread that will always be there.

My senior year, it was time to start thinking about what I was going to do after college. Despite my wild times, my grades were good. I finished with a 3.2 GPA in accounting. Why did I select accounting? I liked numbers, and I wanted to major in something business-related. That is about as deep as that major selection goes. Truth be told, I hated accounting.

As I was finishing undergrad, I thought about getting my master's and even applied at and was denied by Alabama. I was denied because I had to write an essay on why I wanted to enroll at Alabama, and I spent about two minutes throwing thoughts together. That was life thus far, not well thought-out.

I knew enough, though, to know that if I was going to work in accounting, I needed to do two things: pass the CPA and work for a Big 6 accounting firm. In that day, the Big 6 were recruiting hard, committing to students early to make sure they had the teams of traveling auditors they needed. I interviewed with Ernst & Young and Arthur Anderson on campus and traveled to Memphis for the final interviews with Ernst & Young. I stayed at the Peabody downtown, met the team, and interviewed most of the day. In my mind, this job was the perfect fit for me, in Memphis with a Big 6 firm. But, I was young and cocky, with no mentor. I was doing life my way, and so far, I had never failed.

During the final meeting with a partner at Ernst & Young, I was asked what I thought about the firm and the team. Essentially, he wanted to know if I was in. Unwisely, conceitedly, I replied that I needed to talk to Arthur Anderson and compare the two companies before a decision was made.

Really? Who in the world did I think I was? Well, needless to say, I didn't get the job at Ernst & Young. Additionally, the Anderson job never materialized.

I thought that I needed Big 6 accounting experience and the CPA title, but the next opportunity didn't put me on a path to either. I interviewed with a Fortune 500 retail company when they came through campus for a store auditor position. I barely remember the interview, and I certainly didn't go after it hard. After all, I was Big 6 material. As my hiring manager tells it, he was walking to the shredder with a stack of MSU resumes and one fell out of the stack on the way. The one that fell out was mine, so they called me back. True story. What an incredible opportunity to land in my lap, and I didn't even realize it. My dad did, though. He was crazy excited and proud that I could work for this company. I was really mixed, but I had a job.

The World

In my final days at MSU, I remember stepping into the batter's box as we played Wiffle Ball at the frat house with everyone in the field chanting the name of my future employer. Classic memory.

Indiana wasn't the ideal location for me—nothing against the state—but this was where the job was located, so I was in. I began checking out the area and determined I would live in Indianapolis. Kentucky was close by, I was happy to realize. I would be able to go to the Kentucky Derby and see the Wildcats play basketball, both things I had always wanted to do.

But this planning would be meaningless. The hiring manager soon called me to let me know that I could start in Alabama instead. Even better. I would live in Birmingham. Post-college life began.

The job could not have been any better for me to start. It was hard work, perfect for a slacker like me. In those days, laptop computers were not ubiquitous. So, my job was to travel the United States visiting stores. Day by day, city by city, we traveled around the country doing accounting work in the stores.

We had a group of about forty travelers from around the nation converging to take on the stores—individuals from every walk of life, from every corner of the country, as diverse as you can get. It was an incredibly cool experience. I became great friends with people from many different backgrounds. One thing most of us had in common, though: we were looking to have a good time—and learn to be responsible adults, of course.

I traveled constantly, a life on the road that was anything but dull. We would drive out on Monday, work in stores Tuesday through Friday, and return Friday evening. Each week was a great learning experience from a work standpoint but, more importantly, in life. Many stories exist of life on the road.

In Birmingham, I first lived in an area called Riverchase, rooming with an old college friend. We hung on to times of the past. I remember making the three-hour drive to Starkville almost every weekend; I found it tough to cut the college cord. When in Starkville, the normal college antics took over, all-night parties full of drugs and alcohol. I would limp back to Birmingham on Sunday evening, depressed about leaving my friends, knowing college life was forever gone. The college life would slowly melt away, along with the old friends, as I became more ingrained in my company and made close new friends.

In my position, I learned retail from the ground up. I learned what it meant to run a successful store, I learned the mainframe systems that were used to start the company, and, possibly more than anything when I survey today's landscape, I learned hard work. For that, I owe the company a lot. It was a great place to start my career. And, a great way to experience the US.

Johnny Cash sings a song titled "I've Been Everywhere," and I can relate. I've never calculated the number of states that I have been to, but it must be over forty, mostly on the job. From Utah, where we went snow skiing and hung with a hitchhiker, to Vegas and Reno, where we gambled, to Newfoundland, where more people die from moose attacks than murder, working the stores definitely broadened my view of North America. I once spent a week in California traveling from San Francisco along the coast to Yreka, Oregon. Southern Oregon is one of the most beautiful areas I have been to in my life. In the middle of it all, I would steal away for a round of golf with my boss at every opportunity. We had quite the rivalry, both of us bad golfers.

I know how it all may sound, but despite the perks, the job environment was rather intimidating. The work we did in each store was scrutinized every week when we mailed folders back to the home office. Our work would be reviewed for errors. A giant "error board" was kept at the home office, highlighting each error, responsible person, and dollar amount cost. You did not want your name called out on the board. It was effective ridicule. For me, this board was inspiration to do excellent work. My name hit the board once in my tenure, and I disputed the error with a vengeance. It was baloney, but my appeal was overturned by the head of the department. The board served its purpose of creating focus throughout our team.

Life on the road meant living frugally—actually, wisely. We would stay in low-cost hotels and were required to room together. Twenty-five dollars was our per diem for food. In small town Mississippi that was plenty; however, in San Francisco, it didn't go very far. One other interesting fact is that we were not allowed to expense alcohol. All of this taught me how to be responsible within a corporation: take care of it as my own. I remember having my you-know-what handed to me by our administrative assistant for throwing away a paper clip. Frugal, but, more accurately, wise.

After a couple of years, I moved positions and locations, to Arkansas. I drove my rented U-Haul from Alabama to Arkansas, continuing to follow the path God had paved for me.

Rather than stores, I was now on a team that visited distribution centers. We would leave on Mondays and surprise the management team at any one of the distribution centers around the country. Upon arrival, we asked for the manager of the facility and introduced ourselves. The entire distribution center wanted us to leave as soon as possible. After all, our sole purpose was to find issues there. With my happy-go-lucky personality, I hated the feeling of being unwanted. There was no joy at the distribution center upon our arrival, as the management team would be held accountable for findings that we outlined in a report.

Outside of the daily work, though, life was a lot fun. We would roll into new areas and stay for two or three weeks at a time. We always found random things to get into wherever our travels would lead us.

For example, I remember a group of us staying in Minneapolis one weekend. We found our way to a local river celebration in Wisconsin. We rented a pontoon boat and a keg and had a blast. The opportunities for good times were endless when you were traveling around the US with fellow youngsters just out of college and ready to embrace the change that was going on in their lives. Most of us were the same, immature and looking for fun. Nevertheless, with the unwelcoming reception that awaited at every distribution center I visited, I knew that I wouldn't stay in this position long. The great thing about this company was that you could move quickly into different areas, different roles, as you learned the company.

When one of my old bosses asked me to help on the international side of the business, I jumped at the opportunity. I would again be working under him, a friend and awesome boss, and I would have the incredible opportunity to see the world. I would be traveling about 95 percent of the time to various parts of the world.

In the back half of the '90s, international business was accelerating and companies were considering it the next strategic growth area. I was able to get in on the forefront of that strategy. Incredible opportunity. I spent most of my time in South America, China, and Indonesia.

This international gig was right up my alley. I became great friends with my counterpart, and we experienced a life that few have the opportunity to, out in the Wild West. When I say the Wild West, I mean it. The world was not as small then as it is today. Today, many students study abroad, and virtually all students have at minimum traveled internationally. Not the case in the late '90s, early '00s.

We would travel to one area for four to six weeks, come home for a week, then travel back for another four to six weeks. This schedule repeated through the entire year. So, out of necessity, when we traveled to the countries we would immerse ourselves in their cultures. Because our home was essentially in these countries, we would not hang out in tourist areas, doing the typical tourist activities; we would spend time with locals. Their ways of life became ours. This was an amazing experience that has grown a love for international countries and cultures that still thrives today.

Our travels would mainly take me to Buenos Aires, Argentina; Shenzhen, China; Sao Paulo, Brazil; Jakarta, Indonesia; and Hong Kong. At random times, I would visit other locations as well. Distinct memories remain from every location.

My first international assignment was in Buenos Aires, Argentina, opening a quaint warehouse, training the management team, and working out the kinks on the bootleg system that we had created using the warehouse system in the US. My counterpart had the same role in Sao Paulo, Brazil. We spent many hours on the phone together, trying to figure out how to make the distribution centers functional and do life in these countries.

Depending on the country, we would either stay in corporate apartments or nice, safe hotels. In Buenos Aires, Argentina, for example, I mostly stayed at the Marriott downtown. Fabulous city, hotel, and experience. During this part of my life, the people I considered my best friends were in Buenos Aires. I would hang out with them after work and on the weekends all the time.

One of my good friends was from a small town about six hours north of Buenos Aires. One weekend, I went to his family home, and they received me like one of their own. His family had one of the largest citrus farms in Argentina. I remember rising early on Saturday morning and taking the farm help their groceries for the week. The families would come running out of their small farm homes, welcoming us, receiving the groceries.

They didn't have much of anything, but, as I understood it, they were the only farm help with running water and electricity. They were treated well by my friend's dad. It was inspiring to see how he cared for the families.

Family means everything in this culture. My friend's home was modest, with his parents, siblings, and grandparents living under one roof, without air conditioning. But the home was full of the love that only comes from a culture that cares deeply about relationships. In this small community, everyone converged with their families on the city square and listened to a band until late into the evening every Saturday. It was neat to see many generations of a family hanging out, kids everywhere.

In Buenos Aires, I hung out at the Recoleta, local cafés, and coffee houses, jogged through downtown often, and just embraced life in Argentina. I frequented the Hard Rock for the burgers, the closest thing to the United States that I could find. However, my favorite place was Filo's, a hip, artsy restaurant about a block from the Marriot. I still remember exactly what the restaurant was like. It was one of the coolest places I have been, with a great vibe. The closest thing in the States to that restaurant is the Red Bar in Grayton Beach, Florida. I would hang out at Filo's two or three nights a week, making friends with the staff.

I used to love receiving visitors from the United States. Once, my audit friends made the trip to Buenos Aires to conduct their work. We had a blast as I took them around the city, essentially showing them my home. One day we ended up near the river, in the art district, at a hole-in-the-wall bar, taking turns picking tunes on a jukebox and drinking cold Budweiser. As I remember it, the jukebox had a lot of Rolling Stones tunes, and we ended up essentially having karaoke with some locals. It was these random moments in my international life that made my time interesting and memorable.

I am sure great care is taken with international travel in big corporations these days, as everything is so routine. There aren't many untraveled paths taken today. Not so back then. I was part of a group of trailblazers, traveling to remote areas with no international training and essentially no preparation for what we were about to face.

International travel was still new in the company, so we seemed to be defining how it was done. There was no training manual. Prior to going to China by myself, all I was given was a set of about fifty flash cards. On one side of a card would be an English word, such as *McDonald's*, and on the other side would be the Chinese characters for the English word. I would hold up the card to a cab driver, and they would take me to the destination.

I remember once when I crossed the border from Hong Kong to mainland China. There was a giant countdown clock under heavy security detailing the minute when Hong Kong would move to Communist rule under China. Signs were posted all around the area with the words "No cameras or pictures allowed." I have a great picture of the clock. Life was lived figuring things out on my own and trying not to end up in jail or dead.

I did end up in a few dangerous situations, probably more than I knew. Once, in Buenos Aires, Argentina, I was invited to a party in a nearby suburb. My friend wrote down the address, and I was to meet my posse there. On the evening of the party, as I did frequently, I went to the Marriot lobby and handed the concierge the address. He called a cab for me. When it arrived, I jumped in and headed for the party.

After driving for about fifteen minutes, I noticed the lights of the city growing dim. We pulled up to a toll road, which I had never been through, and when I questioned the driver, he turned around and gave me a thumbs-up. I knew at this point something was off.

As we left the toll road, I considered jumping out of the taxi but decided to take my chances. We ended up taking an exit onto a dimly lit street in a very shady area. People, most with no shirts, were hanging out, drinking quarts of beer, sitting on the side of the dirt road. All their eyes were on us as we passed. No cars were in sight, only a few horses being used for transportation.

Here, the driver pulled over and told me to get out of the cab. After I refused, he walked around to my door and opened it, forcing me out of the car. Speaking in Spanish, he then motioned for me to walk down a side street, exclaiming that my party would be there. He left the scene.

So, there I was, in a golf shirt and khakis, walking down the sidewalk, with people whistling and yelling at me. Something bad was about to happen. No cell phones existed in that day, but I saw a pay phone and for a second thought, *a miracle!* I soon gathered myself, though, and realized that I neither spoke the language nor knew how to use a pay phone in Argentina. No cars, no way to communicate, I was dead.

Then, out of nowhere, a car came flying around the corner. I jumped in front of the car, knowing this was my only hope. The driver slammed on the brakes and in perfect English said, "What are you doing here?" I jumped in the back seat and asked him to take me to the downtown Marriott. I remember nothing else about that ride. For this guy to be in this area at this exact time is nothing short of a miracle. I don't want to over-spiritualize this story, but I do know based on God's Word in Matthew 28:20 that God has always been with me. That may have been my closest experience with an angel.

Another memorable story is the time a guy was in Argentina from the States, helping me train some people at the distribution center. We were sitting by the fountain at the Marriot one morning, waiting on our driver. I told him to watch my briefcase as I went inside to grab a cup of coffee. Fifteen minutes later, I walked outside and, out of the corner of my eye, I saw a guy running with my briefcase, ducking into a sea of humanity, the hustle and bustle of people in the city heading to work. My visitor had not done a great job watching my briefcase! I dropped my coffee, and immediately, I was in full sprint chasing the guy. My passport was in that briefcase. I had to catch him.

For about five minutes, in and out of people we ducked, until I was on a stretch with him in front of me, no people. I was catching him, about to leap and tackle him, when he threw my briefcase down. Pouring sweat from the heat, but mostly the adrenaline, I grabbed the briefcase. Just another day in international, as my counterpart and I used to say.

Once, in Indonesia, I ended up a dance club outside the city of Jakarta. Apparently, this club was well-known by anyone who traveled to the city. As I walked in, I was met by strobe lights everywhere, a flashing dance floor, and many eyes following me. Never comfortable, I hung out for a couple of hours until my friends were ready to leave. When we walked out, the "police" began following me. I write police in quotes because they were infamous for demanding money for no reason. I quickly made it to a cab and told the cab driver to step on it. I remember speeding away with the police banging on the cab door, trying to open it. Crazy.

One Saturday, in Jakarta, we took an open-air taxi boat to a local island, one of the 342 islands collectively referred to as the Thousand Islands. The boats were typically packed with people, and the drivers had to be experts. They had to be able to maneuver around the protruding rocks of various islands. We made it to the island, to a beautiful beach, where we took pictures of the many Komodo dragons. Having no idea that these animals sometimes attack people, I got within a few yards of them.

On the way back, a bad storm blew in, catching us in the middle of the rocks sticking out of the water. The captain grabbed the life jackets, the old orange ones, and threw them to everyone on the boat. The waves were huge. They had to be ten to fifteen feet. In between the waves, we were staring at rocks protruding from under the surface. Somehow, the captain was able to steer us back to our dock in Jakarta. Amazing. A few years later, one of these taxis hit a rock, capsizing and killing everyone on board.

The risk-taking and dangerous situations were part of international travel, but these were overshadowed by the fun, jovial moments. After his all-night flight, a guy from Texas arrived at the Buenos Aires distribution center to help me train on the system. At this warehouse, they had a bathroom away from the offices that consisted of holes in the ground where you did your business. There were two footstools over each hole. You stood on them, tilted back, and relieved yourself. Normal bathrooms were in the office area, but these stalls were fun to show visitors. I gave the guy from Texas a tour. "Everything at the distribution center is awesome," I said, "except for the bathrooms." As I showed him the room and explained how to use it, I encouraged him, saying, "You'll get used to it in no time!" I remember his eyes were big. No laughter.

Well, things got crazy that day with work, and I was in the middle of a few fires. I forgot about my visitor, who was out in the warehouse helping where he could. A couple of hours after leaving him, he came by and said that he had to leave immediately. He asked me to please call our driver. I asked if everything was okay, and he explained that his stomach was messed up, he had attempted to use the bathroom on the warehouse floor, and "it ran all over" him. Ouch. I'd forgotten to tell him about the normal bathroom. When I explained to him, I thought he was going to hit me right in the middle of the office. However, he did get me back, as he was the loudest snorer I have ever heard in my life. He slept in the room next to mine, and I didn't get any sleep for a week. Well played, my friend.

In Brazil, one of my good friends once took me away for the weekend to a beach a few hours outside of Sao Paulo. On the way out, we took our car off the beaten path. It was raining, and we almost got stuck three or four times on the dirt trails. I found myself outside of the car, in knee-deep mud, pushing us out. In the end, we found ourselves at the most beautiful, isolated beach that I have ever seen in my life. It was very small and quaint, the kind of place that is not noted on any map as a tourist destination. There was a little hut beside the beach that acted as a store for random boats that came by. I still remember the beauty of that place. The most memorable part of that trip was waking up in a beach hut, dripping with sweat, and covered with about ten mosquitos on me. Miserable, but worth it.

Worth it—that effectively sums up my time of international travel. There were highs and there were lows, but I am grateful for the many lessons I learned. Lessons like, roll with things. Always be willing to take risks, and don't to be so stringent when it comes to schedules, work, and life in general. Always remain flexible. And, most of all, embrace foreigners. I now understand why the Bible repeatedly talks about this. I was one for a season, and I was loved so well by so many that I considered these foreign countries my homes.

During this whole time, there were fragments of God in my life. I used to read Christian books, and I had the thought that later in life I would get serious about Christianity. I never spent any time in God's Word, however, and prayer was something that I still saved for the super religious. But, God is good, and he never left me. He would soon make his presence known.

Threads of the Season of Deaf Ears, Blind Eyes, and Miracles

During this season, from college to the start of my career, new threads took root. Most of these threads were gifts of experience from the opportunities I had. My eyes were opened to people with different worldviews, different cultures, and different ways of doing life.

With all of this change, I learned to mold to fit any environment. I became a chameleon that could perform in social settings or business settings. I developed a thread of keeping things behind closed doors, under wraps. I never wanted to be perceived as being fearful of anything, any person or situation. Reminds me of my dad.

I began to push limits further and further, giving me a thread of risk-taking too. I wanted to be the leader and accordingly pushed whomever I was with to new experiences, new highs, new places. Danger was masked by intensity.

Additionally, many of my threads from early in life began to materialize in this season of discovery. For example, as I mentioned, the thread of working hard was given to me by my dad and the way he did life. Well, this thread manifested itself when I received my first job in college. I didn't count the hours that I was on the clock, as I could outwork anyone. Today's mindset of "work–life balance" didn't exist for me. I just worked hard, playing the one string that I knew I could play.

The thread of alcohol began to show up in the form of binge drinking. This thread led me to narcotics. Negative threads must be controlled, suppressed, but I did not attempt to mask this color at all. Threads were given complete freedom to go wherever they wanted. There was no direction, no vision, no strategy. And as a result, the tapestry of my life became a mess.

When people looked at me, there was little to find of benefit. My example only led them further down a destructive path.
Yes, I wanted to lead and did so swiftly and proudly, but I didn't
recognize the implications of the influence my threads were
having on other people. If I could have understood and controlled these tendencies earlier in life, what a positive impact I
could have made.

But, that is the thing about life and your individual tapestry.
Although your tapestry is a picture of you, the threads bleed
over into other lives. You must handle with care or face regret,
which is never what you want in life.

Reflect on your Season 2

For personal reflection, answer these questions about your journey.

- What are the 3 to 5 decisions that most impacted your life during this season and describe how the decisions changed your life.
- Who are the 5 people that had the biggest positive impact on your life, and what would you say to each person if you could?
- How did season 1 impact season 2?
    - How did your beliefs on religion and God play out in season 2?
    - How did your view of people from season 1 impact you in season 2?
    - Did the area where you grew up impact your journey in season 2?
- What storms came into your life during this season and what was the impact of these storms?
- What threads were developed?
- List evidence of God's grace during this season.
- What was your anchor during this season?
- Looking over this season, what are 3 pieces of advice you give your family, friends, the world.

Name this season in your life.

For a detailed format to record your journey, check out the Seasons Journal.

Season 3:
Grace

For by grace you have been saved through faith. And this is not your own doing; it is the gift of God, ⁹ not a result of works, so that no one may boast.

EPHESIANS 2:8-9 (ESV)

For ten years, my journey had been one of new experiences, new cultures, new views of the world. From college to my work abroad, I had seen the good, the bad, and the ugly. And the amazing part: I was still alive.

As far as success is defined in our culture, I guess I had achieved it. I now had experience that would allow my career to blossom in any of several different directions, and I was with a company that had endless growth opportunities. I was in a great position.

But, for some reason, I felt like I was missing out. My friends looked at my life and were impressed with my travels, my success. Not one of them could match my experiences since college. Many were making more money, but no one had the worldview that I now had. Whenever I was back in the States, attending weddings or parties, my college friends and their new friends would pepper me with questions about my travels. I was on a pedestal.

I, however, was blind to the value of my experiences. In my mind, I was simply behind. As I looked around at my peers and saw blossoming marriages, kids, houses, and seemingly stable lives, I felt like I had wasted the last handful of years traveling internationally. I had always pictured myself married with a house and kids, but I was nowhere near that. I felt like I was a nomad rambling the earth. Every time I was around my old crew, I felt that I didn't belong.

Reflecting now, it's amazing to me that I did not recognize the incredible journey I'd been on. That season of my life was a gift, a blessing. It provided me great wisdom, opened my eyes to possibilities, and developed a foundation that allowed me to embrace the world with no fear. At the time, though, I only saw what I thought I was missing. I was blinded by culture.

Culture will eat your lunch if you let it. Culture beckons you to file in, to do life a certain way, by a certain age. Culture fools you into thinking that there are certain parameters for success. Instead of playing my game, enjoying the journey God had created for me, I wanted to imitate other people and their journeys. I had been given this unique path, but I wanted to be like others.

Longing for something different, I decided the fast life that I had been living had to slow down, whatever that meant. I felt like I needed to move closer to home, reengage with my old friends, and change my course to one that was more familiar. In other words, I needed to mold my life to look like the lives of my friends.

I entered the next season with my eyes set on finding a stable bubble, much like the Mississippi bubble I had emerged from. I wanted a safe little comfortable life. Those aren't the terms I would have used back then to describe my goals, but that summarizes my mindset. And the first step: I needed to move closer to my family and, more importantly, my old college friends.

For some reason, I never recognized any danger in reengaging with my old friends. I thought that after ten years I would magically appear back in Memphis and life would be the same as it was in college. However, everyone you meet is in a unique season of life too. I would soon discover that not one of my friends had a "safe little comfortable life." Like me, everyone else was also feeling tossed about by the waves, trying to make sense of the course they were on, and all were without an anchor.

The fallacy of life is that one can somehow "arrive." We all long for it, run after it, the feeling of success, victory, and unending peace. We mark dates on calendars and say things like, "If I can just make it to this point, things will be great."

Unfortunately, or fortunately, this date never arrives. In every case, success, victory, and unending peace will finally be recognized as a mirage. Only then, when you realize that the world has nothing to offer, will you be enlightened. There you will discover peace. And the interesting thing about this discovery is that, if embraced, you will find yourself on the most daring adventure that you have ever been on in your life. The world will suddenly have meaning. Don't shrink back from the adventure. An anchor is available for the journey.

Simmer Down

The international gig went on for what seemed like twenty years, but it was only about four years. Having decided to shut the door on it, I began looking for a job in Memphis, the logical place, close to home and saturated with my old friends from college.

At age twenty-seven, without a lot of research, really on a whim, I took a job with an auto parts distributor. With my background in distribution, this seemed like a good fit. I painted the picture in my mind that this organization was a small, up-and-coming company with a great future. The money was decent, but most importantly, the job would take me back to Memphis. Exiting the company that had given me my first opportunity was difficult, but I felt this was what I needed to do.

After walking in the door at my new company, I immediately knew it was a bad decision. The office seemed in disarray, and the company was extremely old-school. This would be not a long-term opportunity for me, only a pathway to Memphis and a step toward a more normal life, a life off the road.

My parents helped me find my first house in Cordova, a new area with startup homes, just east of Memphis. For the six months while the house was being built, I rented an apartment right beside my future neighborhood. I was an hour and a half from my parents and some of my family around Tupelo, Mississippi.

At this point, my parents were living the retired life, a gift from all of Dad's hard work. They had moved to a new home in a golf community. Their front yard was a tee box and their back yard was a roughly fifty-acre lake. They renovated the house and built a huge deck off the back overlooking the lake, which offered them a spot to relax and reflect, to rock the day away. My parents spent their days playing golf with different groups, tending to Dad's garden, and fishing. For me, the house was a relaxing getaway from Memphis. In addition to the many outdoor activities, it came with my mom's great cooking. The house was also where the families of my sister and my brothers converged during holidays. We had great times at this house together as a family.

Back in Memphis, settling in at the apartment in Cordova, I found myself in an interesting spot. I was suddenly around several of my old friends from college, but I wasn't comfortable with where I was in life. As previously mentioned, I felt behind, and this was only magnified in my eyes when I became reimmersed in life in Memphis. After all, several of my friends were married with children, and another was successful in medical sales. I was not settled down with a family, nowhere close. I wasn't even dating. I also didn't consider myself successful. I wasn't making a lot of money, and my job was a dead end. So, I found myself in this strange spot of not belonging.

Additionally, during this time, I had minor bouts of anxiety. They're hard to describe, but in simple terms, occasionally, for a few short minutes, my mind would race and I would have this feeling of being completely out of control. This anxiety matched how I generally felt about my life. Sure, I was around old friends, but I was lonely and felt I had no safety net in life, no anchor. Who knew where I would end up?

God did continue to pursue me. There were signs of his presence sprinkled about my path. For example, toward the end of one workday, I remember being approached in the break-room by a local seminary student who was working part-time at my company. He asked me, "If you die today, are you sure you would go to heaven?" I would later learn that question is the classic opening they teach you in Evangelism Explosion, a class that teaches students how to introduce people to God. I fumbled around the answer a bit and finally said, "I don't know." I don't remember his response, but that story points to my lack of understanding of the Bible and my beliefs. I was immature and confused.

My job continued to be a disaster, and I knew that I had to get out. I had thoughts about going back to my old company, and in fact, I called my old boss and received an offer letter from him. However, for uncertain reasons, I denied the offer and updated my resume, believing that if things didn't work out I could go back to my old company another time.

I didn't know where I would end up, but I just felt that Memphis was the right spot for me at this point in my life. My friends were in town, and they offered me a needed dose of familiarity, some sort of lifeline of connectedness that I desired. I guess I was looking for the same relationships and life that I'd had in college. But, as I was finding out, things had changed with the party scene around my college friends. I had been removed from this scene, and it had evolved into something unrecognizable during my absence. Still, I was ready for the good times to pick back up, so I kept navigating this new life, looking for a way in.

The Turning Point

In the middle of writing this book, while on a plane, I received a text from a friend from college: *Please call me.* Never a good sign. The last time I'd received a text like that, one of my college friends had died.

I called my friend, and the news hit me hard. Another friend of mine was in rehab. I was surprised, because last I knew he was living the good life, extremely successful.

I had eleven close friends in college. Among these friends have come two premature deaths, four entrances into rehab for abuse of various substances, and three divorces. I've heard stories too of money loss and job loss. Ironically, one of our favorite music albums in college was *Fun & Games* by the Connells. What seemed harmless, like fun and games to us in college, started a fire that has ended up changing generations. I helped start that fire, and I wish I could relive college, relive those moments with these guys. I wish I could go back in time and point us in a different direction. So many have been impacted, not even just the eleven. Each of the eleven had a wife, a mom, a dad. All had kids. All forever impacted.

I should have been one of those who didn't make it. When I returned to Memphis in my late twenties, my college friends were still running hard after drugs. In fact, they had accelerated their use. I had moved on from the drug use days of college. My attention was on my career, golf, fly fishing. However, having not been involved with my boys in about eight years, I was excited to be back with them. And I was open to jumping back in.

One night, just as normal, a few of us had drinks and headed out to party at one of our favorite spots in downtown Memphis. There we bumped into someone who had some LSD, so naturally, we took a couple of hits. The party continued until the early morning hours, when we ended up at a house where someone pulled out a brick of cocaine. I remember my friend pulling off his boot, hitting the brick to break off pieces, and using a razor blade, creating long lines. We began snorting.

Out of our minds and hallucinating, we continued snorting until about 6:00 a.m. Then, on that rainy Sunday morning, my friend from out of town and I walked out of the house and got into his car, with him driving. I had no idea where we were. Around the Midtown area, I guessed, but my vision was obscured by my clouded mind and the heavy rain. We finally made it to I-240, the loop around Memphis, and drove around and around until I finally recognized the exit for my apartment.

When we made it home, my friend jumped on the couch to crash. Not me. I couldn't. My heart was racing out of control. I paced back and forth, so much so that my neighbors from below came upstairs and asked what in the world was going on. I could not settle down.

Realizing I needed help, I called a friend, and he and another guy came over. They said there was only one cure, so we went to a local Mexican restaurant and pounded margaritas.

I woke up mid-afternoon in my room. Immediately I knew something was off. I stumbled to the bathroom and looked in the mirror, and I was astonished to see blood all over my face. I went to the den and asked my friend if I had gotten in a fight the night before. He said that I hadn't, that the blood was from my nose. I walked back into my room, and what I saw next frightens me to this day. Blood was all over my sheets. I had snorted so much coke, become so jacked up, that blood had poured out of my nose. Not a little, a lot. It looked like someone had died.

There. I got that story out. To this day it is still tough to think about, tough to write about, tough to relive. You see, I overdosed that night. I did die. But for some reason, God saved me. I should have been the third friend dead of my group of twelve. But, I am not. God's grace.

Prior to continuing, I want to point out God's grace in my life up to this point. I didn't get the job in Memphis out of college. If I had, I would have never left the party scene. I did get the job in Alabama—an incredible opportunity at the perfect time in the company's history—pulling me from my friends and the life I was living. Additionally, I should have been dead in Argentina. There is no reason I should have survived that one. And finally, I was saved after overdosing on cocaine. Grace. Man, what an awesome God.

The thing about grace is, you can't make it happen. You have no control over it. It is a gift. You just recognize it and accept it. And, when you do, your life is forever changed.

I wish I could tell you that I changed instantly, that very day my life was spared. I wish I could say I went running to God. But I can't, and I didn't. I slowed down a bit, but I needed help to pull me out of the mire. I just didn't know it at the time. A patient God, though, had plans for me. Man, I need an anchor.

The Gift

The Talking Heads sing a song called "Road to Nowhere" that aptly describes me during this period of my life. I felt alone, hopeless, unsure of what my future looked like. I did not have an intimate relationship with God and never picked up the Bible.

This life was likewise taking a toll on one of my good Memphis friends from college. Early one afternoon, I went over to his house and found him crying. He was wildly successful, but something was not right. Like me, he couldn't explain exactly how he felt, other than to say he had been partying a lot and felt a bit spaced-out from it. My response? "Don't worry about it. Let's go grab a beer." I am thankful I'm a better friend for those in need now than I was then. This friend, sadly, would be one of those to end up dying at a young age.

That night, my friend and I went to the High Point, a bar and restaurant in the Pinch District of Downtown Memphis. A band there was playing cover music from the '70s. As I was talking to my friend, I glanced toward the dance floor, and a girl caught my attention. She was dancing with a couple of other friends, having a great time. I noticed she was doing the "Superstar" skit from *Saturday Night Live*, imitating Mary Katherine Gallagher. My kind of girl.

I turned to my friend, and, completely out of character, said that I was going to ask that girl to dance. So, I did, and life forever changed.

Wait. Go back. Look at those sentences again. I made the decision to ask that girl to dance, and my life forever changed. Think about all the decisions I'd made in life. It should be clear by now that I am generally not intentional about my good intentions. I have intentions to do something but never follow through. This is a weakness, because each decision can be a turning point in life. Each opportunity may be a gift from God waiting to be grasped. I am sure I have missed many opportunities in my life for lack of follow-through. But, for whatever reason, I followed through with this decision.

What did I see in that girl? For starters, she was amazingly beautiful. She was young, innocent, vibrant, fun. The combination of beauty and nuttiness drove me to her. She seemed like a girl I could hang with, a beautiful girl who liked to have a good time without worrying about what others thought.

I walked up to Shannon on the dance floor, introduced myself, and asked her if she wanted to dance. She said, "Sure," and I jumped in right beside her and her friends. My friend also joined our group. To me, Shannon looked like she was about fifteen, so, step one, I had to make sure she was older than twenty. When she said that she was twenty-six, I was relieved. We danced, imitated SNL, and acted goofy all night.

When it was time to leave, I knew that I couldn't let Shannon slip through my fingers. I asked for her phone number. Remember, no cell phones existed at that time, so I had to do it the old-school way, pen and paper. I told her to follow me to the bar, and I asked the bartender for a pen. No pen. Really? Okay, I would have to do it the *real* old-school way. She told me her number, and I committed it to memory.

Now, let's pause for another second. Over one million people live in Memphis across many different areas of the city. If

I didn't get the number memorized, the likelihood of my ever seeing Shannon again wasn't that good. Memorization was critical, I knew. I just didn't know how critical. I didn't know this would be a significant puzzle piece of my future. Memorizing a phone number is a tough task for anyone, and I'd had a few beers that evening, so my mind wasn't as sharp as normal. How in the world did I get seven digits memorized in the correct order that night? I'm still not sure, but I did. God's grace.

There is a rule floating around out there with guys that you wait three days before calling a girl you meet. Supposedly this is to make it seem like you are not desperate or overly excited. Whatever. I'm not sure who came up with that rule, but probably someone who's missed many opportunities. I called Shannon the next day and asked her on a date for the next Friday night. She said no. No?

Apparently, she had started going out with some guy, so she already had a date that night. No worries. "How does Saturday night look?" I kept pushing until I received a yes. I wasn't going to let a little rejection get in the way of our potential future. I would later find out that Shannon thought that if a guy could remember her phone number, she should give him a chance.

The day of my first date with Shannon, I left work to have a first interview for a sales analyst position at another company also based in Memphis. The company needed the experience that I'd gained since college. After the interview, I hightailed it to Shannon's apartment in East Memphis.

My dreadful sense of direction had me driving around lost in Shannon's apartment complex, until I saw her on her balcony. I had not seen Shannon since that night at High Point. She was just as attractive as I remembered; any question I might have had in my mind about that was quickly extinguished. I remember having butterflies as I parked the car.

Having just come from the interview, I arrived in a suit for a casual date. My explanation to Shannon was that I had just left "an important business meeting." I couldn't let her know that I had a dead-end job and I was out interviewing for a new gig. After some uncomfortable greetings, we headed to Owen

Brennan's, a Cajun restaurant in East Memphis.

I don't remember a lot about that first dinner. I do remember that she ordered water and I ordered tea. Shannon later told me that she thought it was strange that we didn't have a beer. It was exceptionally odd for me too, but I didn't want her to think that drinking beer was important to me. Two people in their heads, trying to make good chess moves.

We spent a couple of hours at dinner, then I took her home and told her that I would call her. By today's standards, it was a poorly planned first date. I didn't exactly "go big," post it on social media, and end it with fireworks. Nope. It was a simple date, but it was the way it should have been.

It was all I needed. I was hooked. The best part was, Shannon responded positively when I said that I would call her, and that one date turned into our being inseparable. I mean, every other aspect of life faded into Shannon. Her apartment in East Memphis became my hangout. My house in Cordova became her hangout. We wore a path between those two homes. Shannon's desires became my desires. Her smile became my hope. Her well-being became my goal in life. Her good friends became my good friends. She was my all.

Shannon also brought much-needed order to my life. I was teetering on disaster before I met her, hanging out all night with the guys, and I was in a rut in my career. Shannon provide stability and a dose of joy. I did not have a close relationship with God, so he sent me Shannon. I would come to see the way pieces of my life came together with Shannon in the picture as God's caring for me.

When I think about those first years with Shannon, my mind is flooded with great memories. Like the time we went to the local record store and each bought about twenty of our favorite CDs from college. We stayed up all night listening to music at her apartment. It was a great time spent just hanging out, not focused on anything but us. No social media, no phones, just conversation and each other's company.

By today's standards, Shannon and I would definitely have been considered "foodies" in the Memphis scene. We were always visiting cool restaurants in the area—McEwen's on Monroe in downtown Memphis, Houston's in East Memphis, the Germantown Commissary, you name it. On those dates, we really got to know each other, and from intimate knowledge of each other developed a love that would never be extinguished. I knew she didn't like black olives, preferred silver to gold, and would rather have a simple life than a fake, presumptuous one. She was not into comparisons. This was her life, and she was real.

To this day, Memphis gets a bad rap, but Shannon and I love it. I mean *love* it. The place has soul, character, our best memories. We loved it back then too and leaned into it hard. So much so that after a late night in Downtown Memphis with work the next day, one of our friends declared that they couldn't hang with us too much anymore. We used to laugh at that comment and wear it as a badge of honor. We were young, full of energy, and in love. From hangouts in the Peabody lobby to late nights at Earnestine & Hazel's, downtown was awesome.

If you don't know Memphis, I must give a little more detail on Earnestine & Hazel's, a brothel turned late-night disco. Imagine an extremely old, two-story building with many rooms. Downstairs was a bar, a kitchen that served fantastic burgers, a dance floor, and a working jukebox. Upstairs were small rooms, each with a history that would make anyone blush, one with a piano ready to be turned into a piano bar when the right person arrived. Late at night, people took over the jukebox, playing tunes that kept the dance party going until early morning. Smaller parties and sing-alongs broke out upstairs. This place was just a cool Memphis scene to me. Years later, I would go back and pray in one of those rooms, thanking God for how far he had brought me in life.

If it isn't apparent yet, Shannon and I loved music. We took in quite a few concerts at the Mud Island Amphitheater, ranging from Widespread Panic, my favorite college band, to Sheryl Crow. We saw James Taylor at the Memphis Coliseum. On that night, one of our good friends had too much to drink and boisterously sang all of JT's tunes as loudly as she could. We may have ruined the concert for all of those sitting around us. Then there was the one Saturday afternoon when, on a whim, we took off to the King Biscuit Blues Festival in Helena, Arkansas. On the way back, we stopped at a casino in Tunica, Mississippi. Wherever the current took us, we were game.

Once we became more serious, really only after a few months I think, we traveled to Tupelo to meet my family. Because of the way I fondly talked about my family, Shannon's perception was that they were perfect. I guess at that point in life we were pretty solid, but remember, my family fully believed in keeping skeletons locked away in the closet.

I remember how nervous Shannon was as we made the drive. She was hoping that she would be accepted by this perfect family, especially my parents. She had already met my brother in Destin. Of course, my parents fell in love with Shannon's casual, carefree, simple style. She was not at all presumptuous, like some they knew. As most mothers I am sure, my mom loved Shannon because of the way she loved me.

On the flip side, I first met Mr. Kenney, Shannon's dad, at the FedEx PGA tournament at Southwind in Germantown. He was a hard-working, no-nonsense man who cared deeply for his family. He was a man of integrity. In fact, once, he was burned by someone at his church and mentioned he was wearied of the "double-sided professing Christian." I became friends with Mr. Kenney on trips to Conway, where I played golf with him and his buddies. As for Shannon's mom, Mr. Kenny had divorced her when Shannon was a little girl. That was a hole Shannon always had in her life.

Somewhere in this period, Shannon and I made the decision that she should move from her apartment and buy a condo in East Memphis. (Shannon wanted my help making most decisions, whether it was a sweater purchase or condo purchase, and I loved it.) She would stop paying rent and create an investment—at least that was the thinking in that day. I remember looking and looking until we found a nice condo in an established area in East Memphis.

Once the purchase was complete, we began renovating the

inside, and that was when the condo's quirks started showing themselves. I recall stopping to hug Shannon in the middle of ripping off wallpaper. Sitting on the floor, she cried aloud, wondering if she'd made a mistake. Judging by some crazy neighbors and the loud music that could be heard through the walls, it certainly seemed like it was a mistake at times. But the condo was a cool place to hang out in a great location, and once the reno was complete, it looked great. We spent many hours getting to know each other more at this condo.

By this time, I was in my next job. Not the job I'd interviewed for the day of my first date with Shannon. With no experience as a sales analyst, I had been overlooked for that position. But, a girl on the team had forwarded my resume to a new team that was just beginning at the company. They were starting a demand-planning team that needed my unique experience. I was qualified for this role, having the system knowledge to handle the launch of a program they were considering. I interviewed a few times, and I was awarded the position. Barring the drug test.

The weekend before my drug test was New Year's. Well, as my wild side would have it, I was around some of my old college friends that weekend at a party. I ended up snorting cocaine and dancing the night away with my friends and Shannon. Unbelievable. Of course, I was extremely concerned that the drug test would be failed and my opportunity lost, but somehow, someway, by God's grace, I passed the test. My salary almost doubled, and I found myself with a great company that in the future would lead me to another turning point in my life.

My nights with my old college friends became few and far between. This was a good thing, as it kept me from the drug use that was going on in that crowd. However, I occasionally dipped my toe back into this water. I remember one night I took a hit of ecstasy, and it was very apparent to my future bride. She confronted me the next day and said that I could not be doing that stuff anymore. I had let her down, and it ripped my heart out. To keep me from those bad habits, I increasingly distanced myself from my college friends. I loved them, but it was not good for me to be in that scene.

There is a saying these days: "Not all [those] who wander are lost."[2] Well, some who wander are lost. Looking back, prior to this point, I was meandering through life without much of a plan for myself. God is sovereign, though. He has always been with me, guiding me down the path of life. My first job out of college was in a field that I had never thought about. It was this experience that opened the door to my new company, which led to my future successes. If my faith is ever wavering, I look back at how God has guided my life and I remember how he is behind me and in front of me.

I know some reading this story wouldn't call themselves "religious." Maybe you have no belief in God or think that belief in Jesus is radical. I get it. After all, I don't consider myself religious, as culture has twisted that word. But, in order for you to understand my story, you must understand the role that God and my faith have played in it.

So, allow me to pause here briefly to share some overused, and maybe misused, terms that you hear surrounding religion. The goal is to give you a simple, clear picture of what the Bible says—not what culture twists it to say—and thus an understanding of my life and my life decisions. I specifically want to explain the gospel, belief in Jesus, and the Bible. I know that some will have questions, concerns, and thoughts about my definitions, but this book isn't intended to dive into those areas. I didn't set out to write a book on theology, nor am I qualified. I just want to give you the core of the message.

First, the word *gospel* means "good news," and it is used to describe the life and gift of Jesus. Simply stated, the gospel is the fact that Jesus is the Son of God, equal to God, and that he came to earth. Jesus came to earth because humanity was separated from God by their disobedience, called "sin" in the Bible; he came to become the bridge between God and mankind. Jesus died on a cross, a brutal death, as a substitution, paying the required penalty for sins. Three days later, he rose from the dead, defeating eternal death forever. Now, those who believe in Jesus and turn from their sins receive eternal salvation. The believer is saved from eternal death. This is the gospel, the good news of the Bible.

Sin will always be prevalent in society. We are human. A person won't stop sinning altogether just because he or she becomes a Christian through belief in Jesus. Outside of Jesus himself, a life without sin is impossible. What is different about Christians is that they repent or ask Jesus for forgiveness of their sins. And he forgives. The heartbeat of Jesus is the forgiveness offered to the believer.

One area of confusion with Christianity is in the definition of belief. The Bible is clear that there should be evidence that you are a believer in Jesus. Therefore, belief is having a faith in Jesus that changes you. Followers of Jesus are compelled to live for him because of what he did for them on the cross. Jesus died for them, and believers are committed to this kind of love. Believers will always mess up, but Jesus is there to receive them back into fellowship through their repentance and his forgiveness of them.

My favorite pastor always said, "Keep the main thing the main thing." In this statement, he was emphasizing that the Bible was about Jesus. There is a tendency to focus on different things in the Bible and consequently miss Jesus. He is the main thing, the protagonist of the Bible from beginning to end.

Given all of this, based on the scriptural definition of belief, consider my life up to this point. I had every reason in the world to question my faith in Jesus. If I believed in the gospel, that Jesus died for me, why was there little to no evidence of him in my life? The main thing was not the main thing to me.

Understand, I am not talking about works, as faith is a free gift from God. The Bible clearly teaches this truth. No amount of works will improve one's standing with God. You do not work your way to him. However, there should be evidence of Jesus in your life, what is called "fruit" in the Bible (Matt. 7:16). These acts are a natural occurrence in the believer's life, an overflow of faith. After all, the Bible says that faith without works is dead (Jas. 2:26).

From a spiritual standpoint, when Shannon and I met, we

were in somewhat similar places. We had both grown up in church and made a commitment to follow Jesus early in our lives. However, culture pressed in, and we were not living as if we believed in him. We were not obedient to his Word.

For me personally, I had never studied the Bible intensively, so I was not Bible literate. I just thought God's Word was a list of rules and regulations that might hamper my enjoyment of life. I didn't understand the life principles in the Bible that are invaluable for all people, especially believers.

One of these principles concerns a husband and wife. The Bible clearly spells out the need to make sure that husband and wife are "equally yoked" (2 Cor. 6:14). This means ensuring that both are believers in Jesus. This commonality of Jesus in a marriage creates a binding together of two people. When nothing else makes sense, the couple can run to Jesus and become aligned. However, if both husband and wife have a different definition of God, if they believe in different things, the foundation of the marriage will have a crack. In times of distress or disagreement, each person will run to their own core belief system. The couple will not have a strong foundation to bind them. I am not saying that it is impossible for two people with different beliefs to have a successful marriage, but the odds are just stacked against them. Inevitably, a divide, a significant difference in opinion, will at some point exist that can only be resolved by Jesus.

Since I was not Bible literate, I was not looking for a girl equally yoked with me. In fact, that thought never crossed my mind. I just knew that I was attracted to Shannon, that I loved her, and that I wanted to spend life with her. Even in my ignorance, though, God was good to me. He kept me on his course for my life.

Although I knew Shannon's faith background and belief system, I didn't really care at this point in my life. Even if her foundation had been entirely dissimilar to mine, I don't think it would have mattered to me. Shannon, on the other hand, silently had convictions. She was troubled by the path that we were on. Later, she would tell me how she prayed for me.

Driven by her conviction and my love for her, Shannon and I began visiting a few churches in Memphis. We tried a church named Bellevue, but they seemed "hard-core." Our lives would never match up to the lives of those people. So, we tried a few others. Shannon and I did find another church with a lot of young people attending, and from the looks of things, we would not need to make much of a change to our lives. We could continue living as is and just mesh church into our fast lifestyle. It seemed the best of both worlds. However, we were never settled living "double lives," a church life and a life outside of church. We reached the point that we wanted to be real, authentic.

One day, Shannon and I were driving, discussing church. I remember exactly where we were when this discussion took place. When we had visited Bellevue the month before, Adrian Rogers, the pastor at that time, said, and I quote, "If your religion doesn't change your life, find a new religion." I mentioned this to Shannon, and she replied that she had been thinking about the exact same line. Shannon and I were confronted with the reality that our religion, our belief in Jesus, needed to change our lives. We felt that we had to start attending Bellevue. We didn't know exactly what the change in life would look like, by the way; we just knew God wanted us at Bellevue. God led, and we followed.

Attending Bellevue regularly, under the teaching of Adrian Rogers, we began hearing the truth of God's Word like I had never heard it. Dr. Rogers didn't mince words, and he held true to the Bible, despite what culture said. I was hearing truths I never even knew existed. As a result, my eyes and ears were opened to the Bible in a fresh, new way. I was coming to find it very intriguing.

All the while, all the time, Shannon was praying for me, that I would grow closer to God. And, as time would show, her prayers were not going unheard.

Truth

What is absolute truth? I watched a video once that showcased a number of people around the United States attempting to answer this question. As you can imagine, tons of different answers were received. Many of the interviewees pondered for a while before stringing random thoughts together that led nowhere.

I saw a tattoo once that boldly declared, *There is no absolute truth*. What if this is the answer? What if truth is individual to each person—each person is left to define what truth is, who God is, what is wrong and right, and how one should live their life? In a society like this, there would be chaos, confusion, no order. We would chase money, power, sports, and beauty, and we would try to live forever. Instability, stress, fear, and lack of trust would reign. Laws would not be concrete, as different systems of truth would make regulations of the land obsolete. Does all of this sound eerily familiar?

As I listened to the teaching at Bellevue, I began to desire to know truth. One day, I told Shannon that I was going to begin rising at 5:30 every morning to read the Bible. I had always been told growing up to read the Bible but had never done it regularly. Now, I felt I needed to personally dive into God's Word to see what it said for myself.

The decision to begin reading the Bible every day opened my eyes—ripped scales from my eyes, actually. Each morning, I read in the New Testament, about Jesus and the men who walked with him. Jesus spoke a truth that cut my heart. He was love, a Father who cared for his children. Jesus was not a weak guy dressed in a toga, like I had imagined; he was a leader carrying the truth, with no fear of culture pressing into him. He didn't live a boring life, but a radical one, ready to change the world for God.

And the men, his disciples who followed him—they were committed to him, ready to die for him. They were strong, valiant warriors. The disciples' lives were impacted in every area by Jesus. They didn't have "religious" lives and separate work lives. No, because they *believed*. This was the most important truth that marked their lives. These men believed in Jesus in a way that I had never seen displayed, and in a way that was radically different than how I believed. My life, I saw, did not match their lives or the life that Jesus called future disciples to lead.

As I continued to read, the conviction of the sin in my life was magnified more and more. I began to have a desire to live for Christ. I began to understand what he did for me on the cross and how that must compel me to live for him. The Bible says that there is no greater love than love that drives someone to lay down their life for another (John 15:13). Jesus did that for me.

Our culture has a great misunderstanding of Christianity, of what it looks like to follow Jesus. The immediate thought is that a Christian life means no cussing, no drinking, no fun, no more of whatever it is you consider your greatest pleasure. The focus is on the don'ts. Christianity robs the joy in life, people believe, and this becomes a roadblock to knowing Jesus.

These misrepresentations of God are driven by biblical illiteracy. If I never believed in Jesus but followed the principles of the Bible, I would live an extremely joy-filled life. I would navigate around the dangers of selfish desires, like money, lust, and cheating, and my life would be about loving others, not myself. The principles of the Bible can be used as a guide for life, a path to joy and less stress.

Prior to diving into the Bible, I was duped into believing that my joy came from money, drugs, drinking, living life "on the edge." With this life naturally came selfishness, lying, cheating, and many other sins. My life was a mess. The Bible showed me a different way. What if this God, this Jesus, really changed my life? I mean, what if what I was reading and what Dr. Rogers was teaching happened in my life? What would that look like? What if my joy came from a higher source, not the things of this world?

God captured my heart through the reading of the Bible. He radically changed my life through the reading of the Bible. Said simply, God saved me through his Word. The Bible didn't save me, but the protagonist of the Bible saved me.

Time out. I already wrote about when I became a believer at twelve. Remember? The invitation and my subsequent baptism? So, when was it? When I was twelve or twenty-eight? I don't know. But it doesn't matter, and frankly, I don't care. I only know where I am now. As I said, it took me a long time to be okay with that answer, but I finally and genuinely am.

I began reading the Bible that morning when I was twenty-eight and never stopped. For the record, reading the Bible is sometimes called a "quiet time." That phrase always seemed weird to me, like something you would use for a kindergartener in lieu of the word *nap*: "Time to pull out your mat and have a little quiet time." Whatever you call it, God instilled a discipline in my life to begin each day reading his Word.

I try to read through the Bible each year. Some years I read a chronological Bible. Some years I pick a reading plan that rotates around the books. I read different translations. Additionally, a good friend and spiritual mentor taught me about journaling as I read the Bible. This has become a precious gift to me as well. I have no less than fifteen journals in which I have recorded my morning thoughts from my reading, what

God has shown me. Open any of these journals, read a page, and you can tell what was going on in my life during that time. I can think of no greater gift to leave my kids than the thoughts of their dad as he went through life. In total, I guess I have been reading the Bible each morning for about twenty years. I am passionate about biblical literacy.

Unity

Back to the person who changed my life on this earth, Shannon. We had been dating for about three years, and I knew it was past time to ask her to be my wife. It was time to look for a ring.

I remember going in Mednikow, arguably the nicest jewelry store in Memphis. The salesperson taught me about diamond grades and showed me a couple of stones in the ten thousand–dollar range. I ran out of the store scared to death.

Luckily, a friend hooked me up with another place, in a sketchy area in Memphis. When I went to look at rings here, I had to press a buzzer to enter a small room. There were bars on the window, and the place was under heavy security. Mr. Sam Walton of Walmart has one of my favorite quotes. When someone asked Mr. Sam once about the target market of Walmart, he responded, "Any rational person with money." This jewelry store was the Walmart of jewelers, catering to any rational folks with money. My kind of place. I left with a beautiful diamond for half the price of Mednikow's, and it was time to make God's blessing on my life permanent.

I circled a date on the calendar to propose to Shannon: December 10, 1999. On that day we would head down to a cool bed-and-breakfast with a restaurant in Nesbit, Mississippi, about forty-five minutes south of Memphis, where I had made dinner reservations. As you can imagine, I was extremely nervous heading to dinner. I slipped the ring in my sport coat pocket without a clear plan for how I was going to propose. That was how I typically rolled.

We sat down for dinner, and the whole time, my mind was preoccupied with the ring in the box. While trying to come up with a way to present the ring, I noticed amidst the Christmas decorations these small, decorative wooden gifts scattered on the tables. As we were waiting on an appetizer, Shannon went to the restroom. That was my chance. I grabbed a wooden gift box, removed the top, put the ring in the box, and replaced it back beside the candle. After dinner, I told Shannon to open the present on the table. She laughed and looked at me like I was crazy. As she removed the lid, I got down on a knee. She opened the box and started crying, and I proposed.

The man at the table next to us saw the proposal take place. With a tear in his eye, he bought us each a glass of champagne. It turned out, he was the owner of the bed-and-breakfast. In addition to the champagne gift, he allowed us to keep the wooden gift box. It's still in our possession today, pulled out every Christmas and hung on our tree.

As it should, following the proposal, something felt different in my and Shannon's lives. We were officially engaged. We were now calling our love for each other out, and it was exciting. One of our first steps as an engaged couple was to join the engaged couples class at Bellevue. That was so fun. We learned how to have arguments, how to manage money, and other practical ways of doing life together using the Bible. I can honestly say, to this day, our best friends in life were made in that class twenty years ago. Other couples have come into our life, but none as close as those. I guess we were all tackling life at the same exciting stage. We were married at similar times, had kids at similar times, and learned to do life together. I imagine this was how my parents felt about their church family in coastal Mississippi they forever missed.

As you might imagine, my life looked incredibly different during this period versus just a couple of years earlier. I had almost completely removed myself from my old way of life in Memphis. Honestly, this just happened naturally. As I fell in love with Jesus, my life changed and I didn't enjoy what used to be considered fun. I am thankful that I was removed from that old party scene. I praise God for helping me through that time.

Some of my friends pointed to my removing myself from the party scene as looking down on them, judging them. Not true at all. God just opened my eyes to a different way of life. In no way would I judge anyone. After all, I too have seen and done many things, arguably more than most of these friends. I recognize, without a shadow of doubt, that I am better than no one.

My mindset is best described as "been there, done that." Because of my past, nothing surprises me. This puts me in a unique place of ministry. I openly pursue meeting people in difficult situations and look to learn about the things that they choose to keep locked up in closets. I feel that I can uniquely relate to these people and help by pointing them to God's truth.

There is a story in the Bible that tells of a "sinful woman" who came to Jesus weeping, bowing at his feet. Jesus said, "to whom little is forgiven, the same loves little" (KJV), but the woman at Jesus's feet had been forgiven much, so she loved much. This is my story. I have been forgiven much, so I love much.

Back to the engagement. Shannon got knee-deep in the wedding planning. We would have a simple wedding and reception at Bellevue, and the rehearsal dinner would take place at a restaurant in East Memphis. One of the big decisions for the rehearsal dinner was whether to serve alcohol or not. You must understand my and Shannon's position on alcohol. We have never been against it. In our view, alcohol should never be a dividing line in Christianity. Jesus, the cross, is the dividing line. Other issues tend to cloud the main thing, and as already stated, we must keep the main thing the main thing.

I did not, however, drink alcohol at this time in my life. Some pointed to that as my adherence to legalistic Christian "rules," but that is not the case at all. My not drinking had to do with my personal convictions. To Shannon and me, having an open bar at the rehearsal dinner pointed to our old life, our old way of doing things. We couldn't openly invite this into a celebration of our new lives. So, we determined our guests could buy a drink, but we would not have it on our menu.

We began meeting with an attorney-turned-pastor at Bellevue for our premarital counseling. Those weekly meetings were awesome. They had us continuing to learn what it meant to be husband and wife. I cherish all those meetings, even the uncomfortable conversations. We learned practical things like the benefit of having a hobby together and deeper things like what it means to "love your wives, just as Christ loved the church" (Eph. 5:25).

Even though the wedding was a simple event, its planning was still stressful, especially on Shannon. In fact, at one point, due to the stress on her, I told Shannon that we should elope. I wanted to fly the pastor who was officiating our wedding to an island with us and get married without anyone attending. I'm glad Shannon was a bit more levelheaded about the situation.

In the end, we had an awesome wedding with awesome memories, from my brother getting the wrong color tux pants to my nephew, the ring bearer, grandstanding on his trot down the aisle. The best part, though, was our ceremony's focus on God, just like we wanted. I remember fondly our time of prayer alone at the altar during the ceremony while *Amazing Grace* was playing. God does have amazing grace to save a wretch like me.

After the wedding, our honeymoon was spent in Aruba. Beautiful island and a great time spent relaxing, celebrating, and thinking about the future. We rented a Suzuki Samaria and drove all around the island, finding places to snorkel and visiting local restaurants and shops, all without a care in the world. Unfortunately, we had not yet reached the digital age, and we only made it back with one of our disposal cameras. No worries, though, as the memories are etched in our mind.

We returned to Memphis full of hope and excitement, so happy for the future. As I reflect on this stage of life, I use words like *love, peace, joy, praise,* and *worry-free*. Two had become one, and it was so invigorating to figure out how to do life together.

As one of our first big moves as a married couple, we began looking for a house—one that would not be mine, or hers, but ours. Specifically, we had our hearts set on a house in Germantown. We looked and looked, but everything was out of our budget. Finally, after looking at tons of houses over a few months, there was only one more to see, the cheapest one. We almost didn't bother, thinking it would be a dump needing a lot of work. But I remember entering the front door. After only a few steps, Shannon turned to me and said, "If we don't get this one!" Ouch. That hurt any negotiation power I had.

We were the second offer on the home, so we had to get in line. However, as things dragged on and a week passed without any information from the sellers, I went to work to make it happen. Call it God's will or my persistence, I discovered that the seller's agent was his mother. I warmly talked to her and ended up getting the deal done.

With our new house, my house in Cordova, and Shannon's condo, we found ourselves the owners of three properties in Memphis at one time. A little pressure on a young marriage, but we sold my house and the condo in a matter of months and moved in to the new home with no duplicate mortgage payments. We were off and running.

Our house had all the Germantown charm—old trees and tons of character. We loved it, and we made it our home. Over time, we created and updated the landscaping and enclosed the screened porch to make it a TV room and future playroom. The house was right beside the railroad tracks that run through Germantown. When a train rolled through with an aggressive horn-blowing engineer, it sounded like the machine was coming through our living room. In fact, the first time sleeping at that house, I heard trains all night and thought we had made a terrible mistake. However, what seemed to be a liability at first turned into "atmosphere." The train tracks helped make the house *the* house.

Maybe it's because this house was our first, or maybe it's because we were living there when we had our first two children, but to this day, of the several houses we have lived in, this one is our favorite. It was the smallest and had a bit of an odd layout, but when I think of home, this place pops in my mind. I suspect that is true of all first homes. Shannon and I have so many great memories there.

Life as newlyweds also brought Shannon and I into a new class at Bellevue. We moved up to the newly married class with many of the same couples who were in the engaged couples class with us. I can only describe this class as one that had a ton of energy. There were about twenty or so couples who did life together. None of us had kids, so we had time in our schedules to build relationships. We spent weekends together, took vacations together, and learned about the Bible together from wise leaders with families who had journeyed the road ahead of us. Husbands challenged each other to be the best husbands they could be, and wives challenged wives. We really enjoyed our time together. As I said, the couples we met during this period remain our best friends. With even those we haven't spoken to in years, Shannon and I could sit down and carry on a conversation as though we were never separated. We all were falling deeply in love with our spouses, God, each other, and the church. I can't thank the couples who led that class enough. They were so instrumental in our lives.

Also a huge blessing to us was Pastor Rogers, continuously bringing incredible Bible teaching. I am indebted to him forever for helping Shannon and I deepen our walk with God and getting our marriage off to a great start. In fact, I consider Adrian Rogers my mentor, although I only met him a handful of times.

Bellevue Baptist Church. A Baptist church. A megachurch with over twenty thousand members. With those descriptors, I have just divided Christians, churchgoers, and even those who are not associated with church. Frankly, I dispute things that divide Christianity, because Jesus did the same. Unity among believers is God's desire and was Jesus's prayer while on earth (John 17).

From Genesis 1 to the last book in the Bible, Revelation, we see division wreaking havoc on people. And still today, Christians, churches, and culture fight against unity. In my journey, I have seen a whole host of things divide Christianity. Denomination, church size, alcohol, deacons versus elders, baptism versus sprinkling, Arminianism versus Calvinism, expository preaching versus topical preaching, and on and on and on. I have seen several churches divide over some of these issues.

But for Christians, the dividing line must be Jesus. Keep the main thing the main thing. Jesus and the gospel are where it starts and ends. The gospel is the story of the Bible, and Jesus is the main character. It is all about him.

Rather than religious differences, I cling to biblical truth. Biblical literacy creates unity. Take one verse or one set of words out of context, however, and division is created. No debate or discussion should start with the words "I think." It isn't what I think but what God says in his Word.

After studying the Bible for many years, I see so often how man creates a God who is nothing like the one in the Bible. Rather than Calvin, I believe the Bible. Rather than a particular denomination, I believe the Bible. Rather than culture, I believe the Bible. And, so does Shannon. What a blessing to be equally yoked.

With a solid foundation under our feet, Shannon and I longed to have a family. But first, like most young couples, we decided to start with a dog—a boxer, as that was the breed I grew up with in Tupelo. We made a small list of people nearby who had boxer puppies for sale and planned a day to visit them. The first address was an old trailer in Jackson, Tennessee. As we drove up, we saw one small puppy in a pen. We talked to the owner, hung out with the dog for a few minutes, and then set off to visit the next puppy on our list. While we were still driving down the road, though, Shannon and I turned and looked at each other. "Let's turn around." We did, and Buster became our first dog.

Our family has always been marked by our dogs, and always two at a time. That is our requirement; each needs a playmate. So, Buster had Bree. Buster was an obedient one, and Bree was an escape artist. She could scale a six-foot-tall wooden fence. I had to put an electric wire on the fence. Seriously! When Buster died, we bought Rhett, a black Labrador–Great Dane mix. Rhett was the best we ever had, incredibly obedient and playful.

After Bree died, then came Bandit—a goldendoodle with no shedding who would follow you around begging for petting. And after Rhett died, there was Jett, a black goldendoodle we almost didn't buy because of his energy. Well, he still hasn't lost that energy, but despite that and the disappearance of many socks, Jett is a ton of fun, a keeper.

Outside of the dogs, Shannon and I planned to have three kids, but that was never a definitive decision for us. We would just see how things went. One thing for sure, though, we wanted kids. We tried and tried for a year, but Shannon could not get pregnant. Our friends were beginning to have kids, but it wasn't happening for us, and that was hard.

In order to determine the problem, Shannon and I each went through a series of uncomfortable doctor visits. If you have been through this process, you know what I mean and there is no need for further description. The doctors pinpointed the problem, Shannon began taking medication, and she began watching her "ovulation periods" extremely closely. All romance was gone. We were now trying to have a baby.

While this was going on, my career continued to blossom. I moved to the sales team, essentially taking care of the business of one of the largest retailers in the world. It took a team to manage this load. My first position on the sales team was as an analyst, but I had my eyes set on an account manager position, which would have me leading one of the teams responsible for a specific area of the business.

For the account manager position, I was told that I would first have to leave Memphis to work on the business of a smaller retailer. The thinking was that I needed to train and gain experience before taking on the larger, higher profile role. That didn't sit well with me, as I felt I had the knowledge and talent to do it.

Our vice president, with whom I had a great relationship, left our company and went to Chicago to lead North American sales for a large company. After about a year, I began talking to him about an account manager position. His company offered to let me run a large business, without any additional experience. What an opportunity. The catch was that we needed to move to Chicago, but that sounded awesome to me. I was ready. Shannon was ready to go as well—or at least that was what she told me.

I let my company know that I would be leaving and began getting ready for Chicago. However, one night I received a call from the new company. They had decided that I didn't have to move but could work from my home in Memphis. I immediately let Shannon know, and she crumbled, crying tears of joy. My heart broke as I realized that she never wanted to move to Chicago; she'd just submitted to the opportunity for me. That is my awesome wife for you.

This was the act of an awesome God too, guiding and taking care of us. That reality became wonderfully evident when, a few days after I learned that we didn't have to move to Chicago, the strip on the pregnancy test showed a solid blue line. She cried; I cried. A miracle. We praised God for it. We still have that test, as nasty as that sounds, as a sign of God's presence in our lives. The odds would have been stacked against us and life would have been difficult for us had we had our first child in Chicago without family and friends nearby. God took care of us.

The career move was great. I liked my job, and I really enjoyed the time I spent in Downtown Chicago, staying at the Meridian on Michigan Avenue. Shannon stayed a weekend with me in Chicago once, and we had a blast, with a highlight being the Wynton Marsalis concert at a small venue downtown. Traveling back and forth worked well. However, I knew that to move up with this company I would eventually need to move to Chicago. It was clear now that Shannon and I weren't ready for that, and I wasn't sure that we would ever be.

About a year after working for the company, I received a call from my previous employer. They had been purchased by another company, and they needed someone to lead a large piece of the business. They asked if I would be interested, and I jumped at the offer. It was a great opportunity. Our national distribution hub was in Memphis, so I knew I could remain there for the long haul. I could grow my career right where I was. Things could not have been going better for Shannon and me. Life was awesome.

There was, though, a storm that came during this season that threatened to change life as we knew it. Out of nowhere, as Shannon and I were sleeping one night, I received a frantic call from my mom. My brother, who was living in Atlanta, had gone to get a biopsy done on a lump on his neck. The biopsy went fine, he went home, but he had developed septic poisoning. Things went bad quick. When my mom called, she had to hand the phone to my dad to explain the situation. My dad told me that he would probably not make it through the night.

Shannon and I jumped up, packed a bag, and met my other brother and his wife on the drive to Atlanta. When we arrived, it was touch and go. Things had not improved. At one point in the middle of the night, the nurses were circled around my brother's bed, praying. They said that there was nothing more they could do. I remember my mom and I battling with doctors, trying to get information. I remember her demanding that the doctors begin taking his health as serious as she knew it was.

After a few days, the doctors were able to stabilize my brother. It was a crazy week. At some point, we each thought he would die. But we leaned on God and his sovereignty, our anchor, and he answered our prayers.

Meanwhile, Shannon's pregnancy developed well, without complication. I tried to take great care of my bride and our future child. To say we waited in great anticipation is an understatement. We were so excited. Our friends shared in the excitement, and the experienced parents in our group encouraged us along the way. We went in to hear the heartbeat, and that was the most amazing thing I had ever heard. My baby's heartbeat! It was real! Then the ultrasound came. I just knew it would be a boy. Nope, a girl. I thought I could raise a son, but a daughter? I had my doubts.

Shannon and I wrestled with a name for months. It came down to a couple of potentials. I liked both of them, and we just sat on it for a while and prayed. One day, when shopping for the never-ending baby paraphernalia, a picture on the wall at a store caught Shannon's attention. The pink picture was an alphabet drawing with one of the potential names we had picked out for our little girl. There was our answer. We both celebrated over the name and how it came to be.

Growth

In July of 2003, I was cutting the backyard, when a nine-month-pregnant Shannon called me in the house. It was go time. Shannon was having contractions, and we thought they were close enough together to make a run to the hospital. As all first-time parents are, we were prepared. We grabbed her bag, jumped in our Ford Expedition, and took off to Germantown Methodist, about two miles from our house. We checked Shannon in, and we were ready to have our first baby. Or so we thought.

As Lee Corso says, "Not so fast, my friend." We learned that the contractions were, in fact, not close enough together, so we needed to go home and wait. Crapola. I loaded Shannon back into the high suv (a plug for minivans despite what culture says) and went to get her some soup that she was craving across the street. By the time I came back outside, she was throwing up, in severe pain from the contractions. Being the great leader that I am, I timed the contractions and told her that we couldn't go back to the hospital. She had to tough it out.

When we arrived at home, I paced and timed while Shannon

lay on the couch, crying. She said that she couldn't do it. Being quick on my feet, I immediately replied, "It's too late for that now."

I kept timing the contractions. Finally, a few hours later, we were ready. We sprinted back up to the hospital and checked in, and they had the audacity to tell us that we should have immediately come in when she started getting sick to her stomach. Thanks for that bit of late advice!

About eight hours later—yep, eight hours—we were still in the delivery room. Our daughter was not progressing. The situation was never an emergency, but our doctor gave us a choice. We could either continue the normal delivery process, which could take a long time and give our girl a cone head that would go away, or Shannon could have a C-section and we could make it happen. Hearing the options, my silent ballot was C-section. I wasn't liking the other alternative. I had a picture of the Coneheads from the old SNL skits in my head. Shannon emphatically, verbally agreed. So, the birth of our daughter now had an appointment on the calendar for one hour later.

When the time came, the process was quick, albeit crazy, and then I heard the cry of Riley for the first time. I can't describe the feeling other than complete awe. The nurse immediately brought her in front of my eyes, and I said, "She is an angel. She is perfect." Shannon was behind a curtain, but I could see her face. I looked at her, weeping just as I was, and told her that our daughter was perfect. Experiencing childbirth affirms that there is a Creator controlling all.

As my family grew, so did my faith. I had a good friend at church who continually asked me to work in the visitor's reception area at Bellevue. I had never served in the church, and frankly, things were going okay without it. But, as was usually the case, Shannon encouraged me to try it. I avoided my friend at all costs, until finally I gave in. I would work in the visitor's service area, both me and Shannon. Essentially, our role would be to share about the church when guests came by. We would also give them directions to classes and help them with whatever else they needed.

Dr. Rogers used to say that a church member was either building the church up or tearing it down, that there was no middle ground. As I took the step of serving, my life at Bellevue was jump-started. I felt a part of the church, and I enjoyed meeting the new people, helping where I could. Shannon and I loved it so much that we wanted to serve more. We took every job that came before us. If you want your faith to grow, serve at the local church. Serve the body. It is why we were created.

Growth is the word I would use to define this stage in the life of our family. We were growing in every aspect—in faith, as a couple, as a family, and as members of Bellevue. We were experiencing new things all the time.

Zig Ziglar said, and I paraphrase, once you take a step of faith, things will look different. You will view the world differently. It must be emphasized that you must take the step of faith, though. You can't go from point A to point C without first taking the step to point B. I am reminded of Joshua's leading the Israelites into the Promised Land. They had to cross the Jordan River, which was at flood stage. God instructed the priests to stand in the Jordan and told Joshua that when they did, the river would stop, allowing the Israelites to walk across the dry ground. For the flooded river to stop, the priests had to step in the water. I imagine it was tough, even impossible for some, to believe that God could pull off the miracle. The priests acted in faith, though, and stepped into the Jordan. The water stopped, and a path of dry ground was made to the other side. After their step of faith, they saw the world differently, they viewed God differently, and, no doubt, their faith grew immensely.

I have always felt that the way to grow is to challenge myself. If I envision myself being something, I must challenge myself, make myself uncomfortable, so that I can accomplish whatever it is that I am going after. This was absolutely the case with my faith. I had to trust in God, not be afraid to take the hard steps, and face my fears. I knew this didn't increase my standing with God, however. After all, he is sovereign, and faith is a gift from him. Rather, I worked because of what Jesus did for me on the cross.

So, I was taking every opportunity to volunteer, to challenge myself, that I could. I was reading the Bible daily, and my faith was growing immensely. I loved Jesus. The thought that he died for me on the cross compelled me to live fearlessly for him. However, I recognized that I was not comfortable sharing my faith, telling others about Jesus. That spelled opportunity to me.

I joined a class called Evangelism Explosion. Looking back, do I agree with the process taught? Not really. However, that class pushed me more than anything else in the area of sharing the gospel, and it grew my faith. For that reason, it was awesome. In great summary of the class, each participant memorized a lot of Bible verses and an outline for sharing Jesus with others. Once a person mastered the outline, he or she went out with an assigned mentor, sharing the gospel door to door. The opening question was, "If you were to die today and stand before a holy God, what would you tell him is the reason you should get into heaven?" Depending on their answer, you would dive into the Bible and the outline. Randomly going door to door was crazy intimidating but crazy rewarding.

I know many readers think that a class and process like this is radical, and I hear you. I couldn't agree more. It is radical. But, pushing yourself like this and getting uncomfortable in any endeavor is the path to extreme growth. When you have a fear in life or see a weakness in yourself, press in.

I remember the first time I led someone through the outline. I mumbled and bumbled my way through the presentation, and the young girl listening said that she needed Jesus in her life. I didn't know what to do next. I couldn't believe it. God was in the middle of it, and I was amazed. Luckily, my mentor took over and prayed with the girl, and we invited her to church. She walked away forever changed, and I walked away forever changed. Evangelism Explosion exploded my faith.

Shannon was with me the whole way, praying, supporting, cheering for me. She loved the man I was becoming, grounded in the Word of God. And, she was growing in faith herself, reading daily, serving, helping lead our family to Jesus. As a couple, we were running to Jesus. Two had become one. With God as our foundation, our marriage was blossoming.

One week, the leader of our Bible fellowship class was not going to be able to attend church, so he asked if I would teach. I immediately said, "Absolutely!" See, I had learned to immediately say yes, rather than "I'll pray about it." If you hesitate, it only gives you time to doubt and talk yourself out of it. But, seriously, me? Teach the Bible? I was only a few years removed from my old self.

Luckily, I had already battled my fear of public speaking at my company, and what a battle it was. In fifth grade, I remember having to stand in front of my class and recite a poem that I had written. I was scared to death—so scared that my upper lip started quivering when it was my turn to present. I assumed no one could tell, but my friends in the back row started laughing uncontrollably, loudly at me. It must have left an impression, because I can remember the details.

Knowing that I had this fear, I threw myself into any speaking engagement that I could at work. I was jumping at the chance to lead a meeting or speak in front of a group concerning a corporate initiative, such as our Red Cross drive. Anywhere I could, I would speak. I was able to take a public speaking presentation course through my company, which required I be recorded on video. That was frightening but helped a ton. Eventually, I had worked through my fear, and today, I can honestly say that I really like public speaking.

So, I was mentally ready to teach the class, but it was still a huge step for me. Over innumerable hours, I prepared the lesson I would give on Sunday morning. I still remember that lesson and the illustration I used to teach it. I taught on living a life in "section cz," removed from the playing field of life. cz stood for comfort zone. All of my preparation and Bible reading poured out that morning. I really just transparently unpacked my mind in front of the group. My friends and class members talked about that lesson for a long time and encouraged me tremendously. I came away with newfound confidence in my ability to deliver a message from God's Word, excited about future opportunities.

Please don't miss the progression of my steps of faith. I went from zero church service to testing the waters with the visitor's service booth. Seeing that I enjoyed serving propelled me to take on other things in the church, which finally led to my teaching that class. This progression prepared me for what God had in store for me next.

About six months after I gave my first lesson, the young married minister came to me asking if Shannon and I would lead a young married class with another couple. I gave my usual answer, "Of course." Again, I didn't want to stop to pray or think about it, because I knew if I did I would deny the opportunity. Little did I know what was in store with this class.

Shannon and I began by building a team of leaders. We grabbed two couples who had grown up with us through the engaged couples class, friends of ours we knew were solid, committed, and great encouragers. The two couples we recruited plus the other couple selected to help us lead provided a strong core of leaders as we worked on our class format and launched the class.

I'll never forget those first few weeks after launching the class. Either the co-teacher or I would spend many hours preparing a lesson, ready to deliver and impact a group of people. But there was no group. We would only end up teaching to maybe two to four people. We encouraged each other, though, and kept working, knowing God would bless us.

Early on, we leaders made a commitment to each other. Every Sunday night we would visit young couples who had recently visited Bellevue. Those Sunday night visits proved to be very beneficial for our class and our faith. Visiting these young couples really gave us an opportunity to engage with them. We spoke about their lives, their faith, and how we could help, and ultimately, we would invite them to our class. After our Sunday night visits, our families would gather at a local deli to talk about the evening. We all had a blast, our kids included. They were seeing service lived out.

Finally, one Sunday, about six couples showed up at the class—record attendance! I remember standing outside before walking into the class to teach. One of the wives Shannon and I led with came over and said, "Don't screw this up, Mike." We laughed, knowing that this wasn't about me, but God.

In those days, I prepared my own lessons from my mornings spent alone with God. I would read the Bible throughout the week in the mornings and prepare a presentation between Thursday and Friday from what I had read. I tried to handle the Word of God with great care, wanting to be sure my own thoughts and interpretations didn't cloud the truth. This was about God, not my thoughts. The class needed to hear from God, not Mike. I still have those ten years of PowerPoint lessons I prepared.

God blessed the class, and it began to grow like crazy. We consistently had twenty to twenty-five young married couples in the class. We all became great friends, had great fellowship, studied the Word of God together, and held each other accountable. This gathering really reminded me of the depiction of the early church in Acts chapters 2 and 4. We were a passionate group of growing young families running after God together. We had determined that there was no area of our lives that wasn't open to him. We were all his. It was exciting.

Initially, I thought that the main part of leading the class was preparing and delivering weekly lessons, but I would soon come to believe that was only a minor part. Leading the class more so meant getting involved in people's lives. As the Bible says, "Shepherd the flock of God that is among you" (1 Pet. 5:2 esv). That was my job.

I saw God move in amazing ways in this class, more than in anything else I have ever been involved with. The instances are too many to list, but I'll share a few of the stories that forever impacted my life.

One lady who attended our class suffered from the failing function of her last kidney. She was on the kidney transplant list, and we often gathered in a circle to pray for her. After praying one Sunday, a wife and mother of three kids came up to me and said that she felt that God was leading her to give her kidney. This lady was an incredible woman of faith, but I still questioned her and her husband about that decision. Without a shadow of doubt, they felt led to do this remarkable act. The odds that the kidney would be a match weren't that great, but when God is leading, it works out.

The lady visited the doctor, and, as God would have it, the kidney was a match. I remember sitting in the hospital room, praying and talking with both of the women the morning the transplant was to happen. What a surreal experience. Both of the women did great during the surgeries, and the transplant was successful. I watched the whole process in awe of God and people of faith.

I saw great joy arise in people's lives, but I also walked through great pain with couples. Once, the class gathered at Le Bonheur Children's Hospital to pray for a newborn baby who had been born with a dreadful disease. About twenty couples gathered in a circle praying for the miracle of life, but the baby passed away after only forty-eight hours. We cried with that couple and bore their pain the best we could.

Leading the class had no "open hours." We were always on, ready to help or jump in when needed. One Saturday night, when our family was driving back from a Mississippi State game in Starkville, I received a call from a guy in our class. This was a solid guy, a leader to his wife and four kids. I knew him well. Or so I thought. Crying, he proceeded to tell me that he was in a hotel room in Las Vegas. He and his wife had been in town for a trade show, and his wife had caught him on the phone setting up a time to meet a prostitute.

Over the coming weeks, the double life that he had been living unraveled. The couple separated, and his wife sought God and no one else during the separation. She prayed, read the Bible, wept, received counseling, and, many months after the incident, worked to repair the marriage. I have never seen a man broken like that guy was. But, unbelievably, before my very eyes, God restored their marriage.

Today, having gone on to share their story with countless

others over the radio, at churches, anywhere that would have them, they are at a church in Las Vegas that they planted and have two additional beautiful children. I still have a card with a picture of the *Titanic* that the husband sent me. He told me that when he was living his secret life, he felt like the *Titanic*, unsinkable. On the card, he talks about what a great God he serves—this great God who saved him and his marriage.

Our class was also a generous class, never turning away a need. Once, a single mother of four children from inner city Memphis showed up after one of our couples visited her home randomly on a Sunday outreach event. She was poor, in great need. She had no transportation either, making it nearly impossible for her to manage her family. So, our class did what they did. Among our class, we raised about four thousand dollars and presented the lady with a car. I will never forget the picture of a few of the ladies walking her outside the church to present her the vehicle, then praying with her.

It is true that our days at Bellevue were filled with great works. Don't get the idea, though, that we were trying to work our way to Jesus. The Bible clearly states that works do not save you or improve your relationship with Jesus. Faith is what saves, and faith is a gift of God. However, the Bible does say that faith without works is dead. The truth is that a Christian is compelled to do works because of what Jesus did for him on the cross. Works are simply the overflow of a believer. These works were an overflow of a class wholeheartedly following God.

After belonging to a few different churches, it is very clear to me that God uses different churches and denominations in different ways. Some churches are heavily theological. I was in one such church, and here deep truths of the Bible were taught but very few works could be seen. People seemed to hang on to "expositional preaching" as the key to Jesus, saying, "God is sovereign." On the other end of the spectrum, some churches are light on Scripture, heavy on works. They seem to hang on to how hard they can work for Christ, implying this improves their relationships with God. The correct spot is right in the middle of the spectrum, strong biblical teaching that leads to mighty works. I believe Bellevue and our class had achieved that middle ground.

When I recall this class and our adventures, I am blown away. We were a group of couples fearlessly living for God. Our backgrounds ranged; we were everything from mechanics to doctors. But that didn't matter, because we had great unity, no division among us. We were unified over God, the gospel, and the Bible.

During this time, Adrian Rogers retired and, soon after, passed away. Loved by so many in the world whom he pointed to Jesus, he will forever be missed.

Prior to Dr. Rogers' death, he passed the baton to Dr. Steve Gaines. During a foot washing ceremony, Dr. Rogers claimed that he had known Dr. Gaines would be the next pastor of Bellevue long before the search committee picked him. Dr. Rogers emphatically exclaimed that Pastor Gaines would lead Bellevue into the future. He couldn't have been more support-ive of him.

When Dr. Rogers passed away, within a year of that endorse-ment service, Bellevue was shaken. Some who had supported Pastor Gaines while Dr. Rogers was alive turned on him. Pastor Gaines was called out publicly on ridiculous claims. It seemed like a witch hunt, and it was tearing the church apart. Many left Bellevue at that time.

I remember desiring so much for Dr. Rogers to be able to address the congregation and point them to Jesus. I remember too telling Pastor Gaines that he had the broadest shoulders of anyone I knew for his ability to take the onslaught of rumors directed toward him and his family.

Our class hunkered down during this period. We were all transparent with each other what was going on at Bellevue and never let it impact our class. We continued grow-ing, loving, and serving the church and the city of Memphis. We built a fortress around our people and focused squarely on Jesus.

This time in our church was difficult to witness, a shame. However, I came to believe that God was pruning Bellevue for a future work, and now, from a distance, I have seen it come to fruition. Perhaps some people had been worshipping Adrian Rogers, putting him in the place where God should have been.

For Shannon and me, Bellevue holds a special place in our hearts. Call it what you want—a megachurch or even "Fort God," as it is known by some in Memphis—it is an awesome place. We were married there, our kids were dedicated there after birth, and our relationships with our Father grew tremendously there. This was the most special fifteen years of our life. We always compare where we are to this time, and nothing has measured up since.

So, I ask myself, what was it? What was so different about this season? I can only say that it was two people among a community of people who were all living fearlessly for God. A group of people challenging each other, compelled by the cross. This community developed such close relationships that our lives were forever changed. I thank God for those fifteen years. They were a blessing.

With our church life growing, Shannon and I desperately desired to have additional kids. We prayed for a family of five, but we would be content with as many healthy children as God would give us. One was fine if that was his plan.

When Riley was one, in 2004, we started trying to have another child. Nothing like Shannon's first pregnancy, the second blessing came quickly, as soon as we began trying. We checked the infamous stick, and there it was, a solid line. We celebrated and wept, overjoyed that we would have another child.

I remember it being a lot of fun having Shannon pregnant at Christmastime. Thoughts, presents, decorations—everything was about the baby. We had dinner in Downtown Memphis near the trolley, just Shannon and I, and I gave her two Christmas ornaments signifying her pregnancy. Driven by Shannon and what she did as a child, Christmas ornaments have always been very significant in our family. Each year, pulling out the ornaments to decorate the tree, we are able to remember events and blessings from God. Now we had a couple of ornaments to remind us always of this exciting time preparing for number two.

This is probably always the case, but within me, there was a fear that one of my children would not be born healthy. I had seen this nightmare become reality for other couples, so I regularly prayed for the baby's health. Pregnancy, having a child, means putting your complete faith and trust in God. He is the one who handles the development of the baby, the miracle of childbirth. There's not a lot a man can do.

The only scare we had was around January. Memphis had a dusting of sleet. The roads were frozen, and we were stuck at home. Needing to get of the house for sanity reasons, we ventured out to Home Depot, and as Shannon was walking into the store, she slipped and fell. My heart sank. Helping her to her feet, I was a nervous wreck, worried about the baby. We just handed that over to our Father, though, and everything was okay.

Shannon and I weren't big on being surprised, so we were chomping at the bit to find out whether were having a boy or girl. I just knew this child would be a boy. The day of the appointment, the nurse pointed out the different features of the miracle in Shannon's stomach. Then, she looked at us and said, "Do you want to know the sex?"

"Of course!" we answered.

She said, "Congratulations, you're having a girl!"

I was overwhelmed with excitement. By now, I felt I knew how to raise a girl, so God gave us just what we needed.

Our second girl's name was easy. I'm not sure exactly how, but Natalie Grace came to us quickly. It was perfect, pointing to a God who cared for us and for our baby through the pregnancy. Natalie would point to God. By his grace, we were given another child.

Unlike when Riley was born, I describe this pregnancy as like having a tee time in golf. Since Shannon had a C-section with her first, the remainder would be delivered via C-section. We made an appointment for April 18, 2005, and Natalie was on the calendar to be born. Just like having a tee time in golf, you reserve a time, show up, and have a baby. Well, not quite that easy, but close.

We showed up at five-ish in the morning at Germantown Methodist and went through the same drill. My parents and Shannon's dad sat in the waiting area for the news. Natalie was born and placed in my arms at about 1:00 p.m.

Nothing prepares you for the moment your child is placed in your arms. These are seconds you never forget. Natalie was given to me, and I looked at Shannon and said, "She is perfect. Looks just like her sister."

With our second child, I had another member of the family waiting to meet her sister. I walked in the next room and presented Riley with her sister. She was in disbelief, at first afraid to touch Natalie as if she would break. I remember her holding her sister for the first time, looking in her eyes. This dad was in awe at the whole scene.

Natalie's first night on this earth was a special night. We had a leak in our sink in the hospital room. Shannon was lying in bed, holding Natalie, marveling at God's gift to us, when we had a knock on the door. It was the guy coming to fix the sink. I began talking to him, one conversation led to another, and I shared about Jesus with him. I asked him if he had a relationship with Christ and explained who he was and ended up leading that man in prayer as he gave his life to Jesus. Later, Shannon would tell me she was lying in bed holding Natalie, watching and praying the whole time.

During my thirties, Shannon and I had a blessed life. We were leading the class, our family was growing, and I had a great job. For us at this time, life could not have been more picture perfect. I remember being gathered at the church one Wednesday night with class leaders, praying for each other and the class. I was asked if I had any prayer requests. I literally said that I had none. Life was great; God was good. Indeed, life was great, but I look back at that and realize the folly or lack of humility in that statement.

Business Time

I have always had an entrepreneurial bent and a desire to run a business on the side. I used to tirelessly think about and look for businesses. I remember wanting to buy a nasal strip brand that a company I worked for owned. I felt the brand was underdeveloped and could be grown to be a player in the market. I also seriously considered buying a sporting goods store in Cordova. Nothing ever came to fruition, but the dream wouldn't die.

An avid reader of the paper, one day my eyes fell upon an ad. A furniture business was for sale. I called the broker and visited the business, which was located in an old warehouse. It was explained to me that the owner had passed away and his wife had no desire to run a small business.

I asked Shannon and her friends if they knew about the business, and everyone knew the name, having visited the store at one time or another when shopping for furniture. It seemed that the business was marketed as having great "warehouse prices" on high-end inventory. Most who visited the store loved the merchandise, but the lead time to get the furniture made them buy elsewhere. The reputation of the business was not great.

As I studied the company, I realized the many gaps. The business was not run very well. Upon ringing a buzzer to enter the warehouse, the customer was greeted with a sign that read, *Lead time on furniture is 20–24 weeks.* It took five to six months for a customer to receive their furniture! The company had a lot of obsolete inventory that had been around forever. The showroom wasn't a showroom at all but boxes of furniture. It was a mess.

When I asked to see the books, the owner literally pointed me to a stack of spiral notebooks on the floor. I opened a notebook, and in it were handwritten notes that listed an item, the quantity received, and how many units were sold. I was able to piece together the sales, and from what I could tell, they were moving about $500k each year. Not bad, considering expenses were incredibly low to run the operation. Margin was good.

I brought a friend who had a lot of retail experience into the conversation. He had recently moved states and was interested in small business. He analyzed the company with me, and we thought we could make a run at it. After all, I had plenty of time on my hands, working full-time, leading the Bible class, and raising a family. Why not dive into a business?

Time or no time, the business was an itch that I had to scratch. My friend and I decided that I would buy the operation and he would manage it. I began negotiating with the broker, and within a few months, in 2005, I owned a furniture store.

After the purchase, I met my friend back at the store, and a young employee who had worked under the old ownership was there. I began talking to him about his church background, but more importantly, Jesus. He had a difficult background. We wept and prayed, and he gave his life to Jesus. Great beginning.

Having my friend manage the store was awesome. He quickly jumped in to turn things around. We had to get the business under control, and in order to do that we implemented a system, sold off old inventory, built relationships with suppliers, developed a marketing plan, and hired a staff. Then, once we had gained control, we sought to move the business to a better location.

After an exasperating look around Memphis at warehouse space, office space, and retail space, we found a great location in a population-dense area in Cordova. We built out the space exactly liked we wanted, and our church and friends helped us move in one weekend. We were off and running.

My friend did an incredible job running the store. Sales doubled. We had an unbelievable response to our new location and our merchandise. Everything we tried worked. In fact, we increased our staff and expanded our inventory, and we hired a service to handle our furniture delivery to customers. Our families were involved too. The business couldn't have been going better.

Additionally, we used the space for events, for example, Bible studies and parties. My deep desire was to always use the business as a ministry to others. I remember guys circled around in recliners digging into God's Word together early in the morning.

One guy we had met randomly at church visited our Sunday class, and as I learned more about him and his wife, I realized he needed steady work. He was in seminary, an incredibly wise guy. The business was doing great, so we were able to offer him a job. He ended up being a difference maker, a godly man I would lean on during tough times. He knew the Bible as well as anyone I have ever known, and I always sought the truth from him. God gives us those people in our lives who point us to him. Don't miss those blessings. What a gift this friend, his wife, and their daughter were to me and my family.

The business came to do so well that my financial advisor asked to meet with me to discuss it. He asked what my long-term plans were and described a scenario of "what goes up must come down." He asked me if I would consider selling the business, as he thought it would be a great financial move. The economy was great, the business was thriving, and I could make a great profit. My response was something along the lines of "Are you crazy?"

I was lulled to sleep by success, no doubt. I believed that the curve only went one way: up. This tends to be my default setting. When things are going great, like the business at the time, I believe they will last forever. I rarely forecast bad situations, negative downturns. The business's growth was astronomical, and this would continue, I thought. I also believed the business would lead to incredible ministry opportunities and was not about to miss out on those.

Meanwhile, life with our two girls was amazing, so much fun. I remember spending many hours playing with them on the old screened porch that I had renovated into a playroom. Riley and Natalie were so different. Different personalities, both unique in their own way.

Riley was a thinker, always analyzing everything. We would go to a restaurant and, after sitting down, she would spend five minutes scanning the room, everything and everyone. Once she was comfortable, her demeanor would change, and she would relax. But first, she had to make sure everything was cool.

Her Sunday school teachers used to rave about her vocabulary at such a young age. She could carry on full conversations at two. Shannon and I attributed this to her spending one-on-one time with Mom. Riley and Shannon did life together every day, as Shannon and I had decided early that no matter my salary, she would stay home with the kids. That has always been a blessing to both her and me.

Because of her vocabulary and feedback from others, Riley started kindergarten at age five. I remember dropping that little girl off. The thinker would make me review in detail her schedule. She needed to know everything, including exactly what time we would be picking her up, and make sure her teacher was in the loop on all the details too. Eventually, when she got to be a little older, Riley also became an avid reader and was drawn to computers. She remains one of the most organized, dependable, responsible people I know. Riley is going to be an awesome, successful businessperson one day. Guaranteed. She has all the traits. I would hire her for her organization skills in a second.

Now Natalie, on the other hand, God made starkly different than her sister. If I had one word to describe Natalie growing up, the word would be *passionate*. She always made her presence known, no hesitation in her. She was feisty. Once, when she was about two, one of our boxers licked her cheek, and she quickly turned to the dog and bit his cheek. The boxer yelped and ran away with his tail tucked.

Natalie has always been creative and artistic. When she was young, she loved dressing up and performing. We would put her on camera and she would say "turn it around" so she could see herself on the screen. She and I used to have "dance parties," time spent jamming to Dad's old rap music. We would unleash the likes of DJ Kool's "Let Me Clear My Throat," turn on the strobe light, and dance for hours. Go ahead, Google that song. You, too, will dance for hours.

Natalie always had an opinion, most of the time opposite of Riley's. Today, she continues to go against the grain and be her own person. I see my entrepreneurial spirit in her. Natalie will create something very cool one day, and I hope I get to see it.

People used to marvel at our little family, and now I marvel when I see young parents with two little girls, remembering the time. I would change nothing about those days, except add another kid to the mix, which we did soon enough.

When my wife became pregnant again in 2007, I assumed it was another girl. And I actually wanted another girl, for all of the aforementioned joy my other two had brought to my life and because I knew how to parent them. I read the stats. The numbers showed that another girl was inevitable. It was happening, and it would be awesome. We were so excited.

Shannon was blessed with another great Christmas pregnancy. We had a ball with her being pregnant and going through all the holiday traditions with our two girls, and our traditions were many. They bring back so many great memories. The Germantown Festival, the lights at Shelby Farms, the Christmas trees at Pink Palace. We always bought our Christmas tree at the same local Germantown nursery, where they served hot chocolate and cookies. As a side note, when we bought our very first Christmas tree, Buster, our first boxer, thought we'd installed a bathroom for him and quickly christened the tree.

My favorite tradition, though, was the drive we would take in our car every year to look at lights on houses. We dressed in our PJs, got coffee and hot chocolate at Starbucks, and visit our list of festive houses. In Cordova, there was one home that had a great array of dancing lights synced to music on the radio. I remember sitting in the car with the family, singing and watching the light show.

Around this time, we found a new home in Germantown. It was tough to leave that first home. As I said, we still call that very first home our favorite. So many memories. But, our new home had the same old trees, a larger yard, and more room for a growing family.

This was also about the time we found out the sex of the baby. I remember the shock I experienced when the nurse said, "You are having a boy." What? I was stunned. I suddenly shifted my mind to what this meant. This would be interesting.

The name came down to Caleb or Griffin. Except, Natalie had her own name for her future brother. She seriously named him "Johnny Puke." When we were around friends, they would playfully ask what her brother's name was, and the four-year-old would proudly exclaim, "Johnny Puke!" As the days went on, the name Griffin stuck with the girls, and it was settled. It couldn't have been more perfect for him.

Griffin's delivery was another put on the calendar like a tee time, scheduled first thing in the morning. Again, like most parents, I was just praying for a healthy baby. Part of me was full of paranoia that there was no way I could have three healthy kids. Even as I type this, a tear wells up in my eye as I think about the miracle of childbirth.

The moment I laid eyes on my son, I was forever his. For the third time, I looked at Shannon behind the curtain in that delivery room and told her, "He is perfect." I took Griffin and held him by Shannon's head as she wept tears of joy.

I remember the celebration with the girls outside, complete

madness. However, the madness was just beginning. The day that we brought Griffin home, Shannon was changing his diaper and he sprayed Natalie. Yep, no doubt about it: life would be different from now on.

Natalie's best friend was the son of our best friends. They were the same age and were pretty much brother and sister. I thought that there had never been such a destructive person in the world as that boy—that is, until Griffin came along. At one point, Shannon and I asked each other if this was normal. The truth glared at us that girls are girls and boys are beasts. There were still dance parties, sure, but there was also wrestling, football, basketball, anything that Griffin could think of that involved a ball or simply two kids hitting each other. Throwing him in the mix changed things.

I didn't have to teach my son to like sports, camouflage, fishing, hunting, or guns. Griffin came out with a good chunk of Mississippi blood in him. We went on hikes in the woods by our house, fished at lakes near our house, and played ball. Once, I remember sitting, holding my knees with my fishing pole next to me, waiting on a bite. I looked about twenty yards away, and Griffin was in the exact same position, holding his knees with his fishing pole beside him. That moment impressed on me so much the importance of living my life fully committed to God to emulate what it looks like. If Griffin wanted to be like me, I wanted to be like Christ. In one of his letters, the apostle Paul told his mentees, "Be imitators of me, as I am of Christ" (1 Cor. 1:11). That is my prayer for Griffin.

Actually, my prayer for Griffin that we recite several times together each week is Romans 12:2: "Do not copy the behavior and customs of this world, but let God transform you into a new person by changing the way you think. Then you will learn to know God's will for you, which is good and pleasing and perfect" (NLT). I'll say part of the verse, stop in a random place, and my son will repeat the rest. Don't conform, Griffin.

As the Bible says and as I have mentioned, there is no greater love than when a man lays down his life for another. I always tell my kids that I would die for them, and I would. I will do my best to emulate Jesus for them. As a reminder, I ask my kids, "How much do I love you?" and they respond, "All day, all day." That exchange originated when they were little ones, and I use it today to remind them how much I love them.

I can't write about this time in my life without writing about our favorite place on earth. Growing up, quite a few of my vacations were spent in the Destin, Florida area, and in college I took many trips there too. The vacation tradition continued with our family. From 1999 to 2017, we went to the Destin, or 30A, area every year. Because of this consistency, we have tons of memories with our kids there. Our kids know the communities like the back of their hand, and they each have their favorite spots and stories. We were in the middle of 30A before it became known as 30A. Because of the growth and popularity of the area, our vacations slowly moved down the beach, away from the crowds, finally settling in the Rosemary Beach and Inlet Beach areas.

When we're in town, we park our cars and ride bikes most of the week. Everyone in the family has a favorite restaurant that we visit, like the Red Bar or the Local Catch or the Seagrove Village Market Café.

We have a relationship with the lady who started the infamous Sugar Shak. Before it became so popular, our family would sit in front of the then tiny store and swing on the front porch swing. The original owner has since sold the business, and today, you can barely get in the large store because of the popularity of the old-school candy and the ice cream.

One of our favorite activities is renting a pontoon boat and spending the day on and around Shell Island gathering starfish and seashells and fishing. We always seem to bump into interesting sea creatures. Once, we had a large manatee swim by us as we were snorkeling, and another time, a hammerhead shark came within five yards of all the girls while they were in the water.

So many memories flood my mind, such as being at the beach when 9/11 happened. I remember watching the towers come down in shock, going out to the beach, and seeing planes fly over us in fighter formation, as the area is near a base. Just driving down 30A to this spot enters me into a complete state of relaxation, reflection, and inflection. If we are on vacation, you can find us near the Seacrest Beach, Rosemary Beach, and Inlet Beach area. This will always be our favorite spot in this world.

Changing Times

The year 2008, the year Griffin was born, was marked by a booming economy and quality of life. My career continued to blossom as I continued to take on additional responsibilities. My side business was also growing. Sales were zooming, we expanded, and we were considering leasing another building that would more than double our space.

My ministry at Bellevue was thriving too. The class was incredibly close. We were always pushing each other toward deeper relationships with Christ and leaning on each other through the tough times. My growing family really benefitted from the ministry. We had a group of couples we did life with, and these people were like extended family members to us. Our kids were close to their kids, and we were close to them.

Now into my and Shannon's late thirties, life still could not have been any better in our estimation. When I reflect on these times, I thank God for the blessings and experiences. Everything was clicking on all cylinders. In fact, if we were to rank our seasons in life, this would be at the top of the list. These were special times, indeed.

However, the funny thing about great seasons in your life is that you lull yourself into thinking they will last forever. They will not. Count your blessings, enjoy seasons and moments in life that are peaceful and promising, because they will come to an end.

This season was about to come to an end for us. As we were enjoying life, storms were forming ahead of us that we couldn't see. And once they hit, life would never be the same as in the past ten years.

If you are in your own season of plenty, if you feel things are going perfectly and can scarcely think of a prayer for yourself, recognize that eventually, a storm will come. The earlier you recognize this, the better you will be able to steady the ship when the water gets rough. Be prepared. Find your anchor. You will need it.

In October 2008, things began to change in the United States. The housing market crumbled, the bubble burst, a "recession" began. I put this word in quotes, because, in a lot of ways, the Harveys never felt it. Sure, retail sales struggled a bit, but my company remained solid. My career never stopped soaring.

However, our small business was a different story. People began to frugally manage their money, and like the entire retail sector in the United States, our business suffered tremendously. Sales were down about 20 percent.

Still, we felt we had our legs under us. We began to market heavily, and we partnered with local companies and located any incremental revenue we could find. All the while, I continued to operate as an absentee owner, flying very high at a strategic level, keeping an eye on the financials. I had great people running the store.

In 2009, with our sales and the economy seemingly stabilizing, we began discussing and praying about expanding the business to other markets. We wanted to open in Nashville, but another store owned that market. After failed attempts at trying to partner with this company, we began to look at other markets, finally circling Jackson, Tennessee, about ninety miles east of Memphis.

We found a spot to lease, and our assistant manager in Memphis agreed to move to Jackson to open the store. I felt great pressure moving him and his family to Jackson. They had a tough time fitting into the new culture. As I would find out later in life, moving towns isn't easy. Not only did his family struggle, but the Jackson location never gained footing. I can point to a lot of reasons, but overall, I believe the market was not large enough to support the store.

I try my best in life not to second-guess my decisions, but this one didn't work out. It was a depressing ride for about a year, draining cash from our Memphis store and me personally. We finally closed the store and moved everyone back to Memphis to focus on our home location. Unfortunately, the drain on the business from the Jackson store continued to cause strain in Memphis.

This was difficult for me, but really, apart from the business, things were still good. God was working in my life in amazing ways. I continued to glean from his Word and grow spiritually. Our family was doing great as well. Great career, great friends, great church, healthy kids—everything was awesome.

But, this troubled me. I felt that I was living in this safe little bubble. When I read about the people in the Bible, I was so convicted to give Jesus my all. When I thought about what he did on the cross for me, I was compelled to go wherever, do whatever for him. Was I fully acting on that, though? Was I giving God my all?

David Platt wrote the most challenging book I have ever read, *Radical*, during this time. In it, Platt essentially emphasizes the Bible and how it defines living for Christ. Fair warning: never read the Bible for a "light read." The Bible is challenging, convicting, life-changing. I always say that there is nothing reactive about the Bible. The Bible is a proactive action book. So, pointing directly to Scripture, not his thoughts, Platt in *Radical* demonstrates that a life lived following God is not what we would call a safe life. A life lived following God is about others. This journey will take you places that you never envisioned. Aspirations will be less about your own personal well-being and more about the well-being of others.

As I dove into *Radical* with my wife and our Bible class, more and more on my mind was how to use my furniture business for the world. Sure, I wanted the business to be profitable, but ultimately, I wanted to use the business as a ministry to help others. I never knew what this could look like, but a new phrase, at least to me, started floating around: "business as mission." I began studying and reading about what it meant to use a business as a mission. This led me to explore the world of microfinancing and think about what it could look like using the business as the backing for small international loans.

One morning while I was reading the Bible, a verse that I had read a hundred times stopped me in my tracks. It was James 1:27, which says, "Pure and genuine religion in the sight of God the Father means caring for orphans and widows in their distress and refusing to let the world corrupt you" (NLT).

I heard John Piper preach a sermon once about God's having specific verses for different people. He will change your life through his Word. So, when I say that the verse stopped me in my tracks, I mean that the verse changed my life.

The phrase "caring for orphans" was magnified on this morning. I felt that was the answer to what God wanted me to do with the business. God wanted me to care for orphans, a crazy thought at the time. Sure, I always cared about kids, and my own children strengthened the compassion, but adoption or other involvement with orphans? As I remember it, this thought had never been on my mind. I had been thinking about how to alleviate poverty, not care for orphans.

As the days went on, I began to see a thread in the Bible. God repeatedly talks about caring for three groups of people: foreigners, widows, and orphans. These are three groups of people who are completely helpless, three groups of people who can't give you anything in return. The call was very clear on my life and the business. The business was to be used to care for orphans.

So I had a vision, but I had no clue how to move forward.

I was praying, talking to people, and reading the Bible. I met with ministers, friends, and people who ran ministries, looking for a path to care for orphans. This went on, and it came time for the Bellevue Missions Fair, a time when speakers and missionaries educated the church about their specific ministries. The speakers and missionaries would set up booths throughout the church, highlighting their ministries, and you could spend personal time getting to know the missionaries one-on-one.

As I was walking through the halls, scanning the different booths, I noticed one booth that had a sign with James 1:27 on it, the very verse God had used to change my life. I quickly walked up to the booth, introduced myself, and learned about the organization. They essentially cared for about ten orphanages worldwide. They were set up to pass through 100 percent of donated funds to these ten orphanages. Said differently, if I donated $100 to an orphanage, $100 would go to the orphanage. There were no administrative fees. It was an awesome model. I asked the girl working the booth if I could meet the founder, and she gladly gave me his name and number.

I could not wait to talk to him. I had been wandering for six months trying to find out how God wanted me to use my business and my life caring for orphans, and I now had found an organization with the same mission. I called the founder that Sunday afternoon and told him that I would like to meet with him to talk about a potential partnership and learn about his ministry. He told me that he was in the Amazon and would not be back for three weeks. He asked if we could meet for lunch when he got back in town. I remember thinking, *Three weeks! How can I wait three weeks?*

Follow

The three-week wait was excruciating. But finally, I was having lunch with the founder of an outstanding organization.

To begin our conversation, he briefly told me about the ministry and how he had just returned from visiting a newer orphanage in Southern Colombia. He then asked me what was on my mind. I recounted my journey, how God had led me to James 1:27 and how I'd recognized this verse on the booth. I told him about my business, how I believed that God wanted me to use it as a mission, and how I was now searching for a partner.

Immediately, the founder replied by asking me if I would go on a trip with him in a few weeks. The question startled me, as I knew he was about to ask me to do something uncomfortable. He asked me to go with him to Leticia, Colombia, a small city in the middle of the Amazon jungle on the Amazon River. Not wanting to back down from where I believed God was leading me, and never willing to fall into the trap of "taking time to pray about it," I looked him square in the eyes and said, "I am in."

As I walked out of that restaurant, I felt I was out of my mind. Colombia? All I knew about Colombia was that it was extremely dangerous, full of kidnappings and drugs. Of all places, God, why Colombia? I would gladly go to Honduras or one of the closer, better-known countries. Why start with Colombia? I remember telling my faith-filled wife, and she was excited for me. She wasn't worried a bit about Colombia. Her trust was in God.

I began to get to know the ministry over the next few weeks as well as the plans for this specific trip. On the trip, I would be going with a few people from a church in another state. I got to know them a bit over the phone, and I convinced myself that if these normal people—a pastor, a doctor, and a teacher—were going to Colombia, I could go. So, the trip was set. I would be heading to the Amazon jungle.

Prior to the trip to the jungle, we had a vacation planned with the family in Florida. We went with good friends for two weeks. The first week, the husbands would be there, and the wives would stay an extra week with the kids. As it turned out, my friend, the dad of the other family, couldn't go, as he was in the Army Reserve and had to work an area where a hurricane had recently hit.

I would find myself unable to enjoy that vacation, as Colombia was on my mind. To say I was nervous and over-whelmed is an understatement. I had gone from a guy who would not work the visitor's booth at church to a guy who was heading to Colombia to work with orphans.

I remember leaving my family in Florida after the first week, kissing them goodbye and feeling like I would never see them again. This is the honest truth. I felt that I would never see them again. I guess I was learning what it meant to follow God. He never calls us to our safe comfort zone. He challenges.

When I arrived back in Memphis, I had a few days to get my work straight and prepare for the trip. Those were lonely days. I prayed, read the Bible, and deepened my dependency on God.

The day before my trip, I went to Walmart to pick up some suggested items: a flashlight, insect repellant, sunscreen, and snacks. After I pulled into the parking lot, I sat in my car and began to pray. I soon found myself crying as I told God that I felt alone, I was scared, and I needed him. My fear was driven by the fact that I did not believe that I would see my family again.

I prayed for each member of my family, starting with Shannon, then the kids. In my mind, I handed my kids over to God. I told him, "They are yours." I vividly remember a thought of his saying to me, "Finally! I can handle your kids much better than you." I told God that I needed some encouragement. I literally felt like I was going insane, talking to myself, crying, desperate for hope.

I finished my prayer by praying more specifically for a person to encourage me. Then, I stepped out of my car, fully expecting to bump into someone from my Bible class. I just knew God would help me. Instead, as I was walking into Walmart, a guy walked right in front of me, cutting me off and stopping me in my tracks, and acted as if he didn't see me. How rude. I went in the store, gathered the recommended items for my trip, and found my place in a long checkout line. I was shaken and empty.

While I was standing there, a guy standing a few people in front of me turned around and called out, "Where are you headed?" I thought he was crazy. I quietly responded that I was going on a trip, all the while thinking, *Settle down, brother. Stop being so loud!*

Well, the guy apparently didn't get enough information from my response. He stepped out of line and moved back in line beside me. He said that he saw my insect repellant and was wondering where I was going. I should buy the clip-on version, he said. It worked great.

Is this really happening? I thought. *Please just leave me alone.*

He continued asking me about my trip, and I told him that I was going on a mission trip. He asked, "Where?" When I told him Colombia, his eyes lit up.

I, then, recognized the strange guy. He was the one who had walked in front of me when I was entering the store.

He went on to tell me that he had been going on mission trips to Venezuela, a country neighboring Colombia. He told me all of the remarkable ways he had seen God working. He was an optometrist who took glasses to the poor, literally changing people's lives giving the gift of clear vision. As he told me the story about this one little girl who had not been able to see prior to receiving glasses, he began to tear up. Listening, I began to tear up too.

By the time we arrived at the register, we were both so shaken that I am not sure who paid for what. I heard a few more stories before we parted ways, and I told him that God had sent him to encourage me.

That exchange was one of the most amazing ways I have seen God immediately answer a prayer in my life. After that visit, I was all in. I now knew the truth of Matthew 28:20, where Jesus says that he is always with us, and I knew what Job meant in verse 42:5 when he says, "My ears had heard of you but now my eyes have seen you."

I thought that God had literally sent an angel to minister to me, but years later, I would bump into this same man, around the same place in that same Walmart. On that day I stopped him and asked him if he was an optometrist who took mission trips to South America. He affirmed my guess. When I told him how he had blessed me, however, he was perplexed. He doesn't remember that conversation a bit. God works in mysterious ways.

On my trip to Colombia, I kept a detailed daily journal, a habit that I have tried to practice during key moments in my life. My stated purpose for the trip as written in my journal was,

God gave me a vision for my business through James 1:27, caring for orphans in their distress. The business will be utilized to glorify God by caring for orphans in their distress. I have been praying for my next step with the business, and God led me here.

I then wrote,

The second piece of the vision was to lead family mission trips through our business, trips to the orphanage. This trip is the beginning.

The trip really served as a monumental time in my life. It would change the course for me and my family forever.

I was incredibly nervous on that plane ride to Colombia, not understanding exactly where I was going or knowing who I was going with. I was just doing my best to follow and listen to God.

God gave me the following verses to keep in my mind on this trip, all through my morning reading of the Word. I share these so that you see the practical, invaluable encouragement received from spending time alone with God.

- Psalm 56:3 – When I am afraid, I put my trust in you.

- Psalm 1:6 – For the Lord watches over the way of the righteous.

- Psalm 62:5–6 – Let all that I am wait quietly before God, for my hope is in him. He alone is my rock and my salvation, my fortress where I will not be shaken. (NLT)

- Psalm 37:23–25 – The Lord directs the steps of the godly. He delights in every detail of their lives. Though they stumble, they will never fall, for the Lord holds them by the hand. Once I was young, and now I am old. Yet I have never seen the godly abandoned or their children begging for bread. (NLT)

- Matthew 28:20 – "Surely I am with you always, to the very end of the age."

The Bible is a gift from God. He has spoken and continues to speak through his Word. Never take this gift for granted. God will change your life through biblical literacy.

In the Bible, God says that he does not change. He is the same yesterday, today, and forever. His Word stands. I needed something that did not change. My life was changing now very quickly. The economy had evaporated before me eyes, and stability was hard to come by. God and his Word were my anchor.

Colombia

On June 24, 2010, on the airplane to my layover in Atlanta, Georgia, I wrote a note to my family in large ink that read,

Hello! I love you, Shannon, Riley, Natalie, and Griffin. Bye bye.

I snapped a picture of the note and sent it to Shannon. I literally did not think I would return to Memphis or see them again. My journal entry for June 24 begins,

I left Memphis this morning confident God was going to do a good work. I knew he was in control, but I was scared to death.

I met the team in Atlanta and began the journey to Leticia. We overnighted in Bogota, a metropolis of fifteen million people. Bogota is vibrant, full of energy. I could live there. That first morning, I led the devotional, talking about Jesus's cry of unity in John 17 and following.

After the devotional, I began to learn more about Leticia and La Aljaba. Leticia is Colombia's southernmost town and its only major port on the Amazon River. Leticia has about forty thousand inhabitants on the northern bank of the Amazon and is located at the point where Colombia, Brazil, and Peru come together in an area called Tres Fronteras (Three Frontiers).

The city of Leticia presents many opportunities and challenges, on account of the location, education, and culture of the community. With the city's location in the middle of the Amazon jungle, the community can only be reached by plane or boat via a month-long trip up the Amazon River. Unemployment is estimated at about 75 percent. With this unemployment rate, it is easy to imagine the poverty situation in the community. The lucrative drug trade in Peru pulls many youths from Leticia. Many poor people graduate high school and head to Peru or Brazil to work in the cocaine market and other illegal businesses.

Population growth has been quoted at above the 20 percent level in Leticia and Tabatinga, Brazil, the city that borders Leticia. The Tabatinga–Leticia region is expected to grow from seventy thousand to one million people by the year 2022. With this growth, a housing problem has arisen. The city currently has a housing deficit of at least 4,900 units. The local economic structure was not built to handle the population growth. In addition, vacant land is very difficult to find. The city is land-locked, with the only room for expansion being north of Leticia into mostly uncleared jungle areas.

The need for an orphanage is great, as children in Leticia face many threats. Dangers for children in Leticia include abandonment, abuse, health, poverty, and sexual slavery. These are worldwide issues—specifically, human trafficking is a major issue in the world, ranked as the number two crime in the United States—but God had put Leticia in my path.

The mission statement of the orphanage in Leticia is to "assist abandoned, orphaned, and poor children offering assistance in four development areas: physical, cognitive, spiritual, and emotional well-being." The vision is "under inspiration of God's love and obeying his calling, to impact the Amazon community by teaching Christian values and principles to the children for future generations." The home provides for children from four to eighteen years of age in situations of extreme poverty or need. It opened in April 2004, the full-time effort of a local missionary, with eight children. Five of these had been abandoned by their mother, and three were in situations of poverty. Today, the home provides a full daycare, tutoring, and daily nutritious meals for about seventy-five children, and they provide twenty-four-hour care for about twenty-six children.

Landing in Leticia, I was immediately hit by how hot it is by the equator. (Truth be told, not a lot different than Memphis in the summer.) More than that, though, it was impressed upon me how far God had taken me. I couldn't believe it. How awesome. There was so much more to come, though. What I experienced that trip literally changed my worldview, my life, my mission in life.

At the orphanage, I found that the kids were radically different than kids in the US. They all got along, not one argument among them. They were appreciative with what they had and shared with each other. The orphanage was incredibly positive, not a dark, sad place at all.

Language was not a barrier, as love has no language. While we were walking to a local pizza restaurant one night, one shy girl, about ten, walked up and grabbed my hand as we walked. Those kids just want to be loved and accepted. I was thankful for the security that they had in Jesus and at the orphanage.

That trip, I was able to help the home by funding a project with our business, a room addition connected to the orphanage. The new room would be used to house visitors when they came to stay with the kids. I was so thankful that God had led me here and that I was able to direct profits of the business toward missions. This was my dream, my vision that began with James 1:27. And it wouldn't stop here. After this first trip, God would work to cement the vision he had placed in my heart.

When you follow God, hang on. It is never boring. Now would be a great time to quote my favorite line by the Grateful Dead: "What a long, strange trip it's been."[3]

When I returned to Memphis, I settled back in to find that my restlessness, that feeling that something was missing in my life, hadn't been settled. All areas of my life were continuing to flourish. My career was still growing. Our furniture business remained flat but still seemed sustainable. My marriage was great. I had three healthy kids. And the Bible class I led at church was strong. Truly, I was blessed beyond belief.

Honestly, I could have stayed in this safe little bubble. I could have retired early and moved to a beach house in Florida as God continued to rain down blessings. However, this didn't feel right. I knew that life was about greater things than my temporary joy on this earth. God had other plans for me. I knew this deep down, but I just didn't know exactly what it looked like. The vision he had put in my heart that led to Colombia continued to swirl in my mind, my heart.

Shannon took a trip to the orphanage the next year. She wanted to see what I had seen. She, too, came back with a vision of how the Harvey's could help. I remember a few months after her trip, I was driving down a Mississippi back road with her and she broke down in tears, telling me that she was thinking about the kids at the orphanage. Our lives had been changed forever.

The manager of my store also took a trip to the jungle, having himself gained a desire for the business to be used directly for this mission. We began praying, talking, and planning what we might be able to give to the orphanage each month. We settled on an amount and worked that into the store's budget. I remember standing in a circle with three couples praying through this amount and all walking away in tears, knowing what we were to give. The amount was overwhelming, but we felt we needed to trust. The danger that existed in Leticia for the kids was real and had been cemented in our minds.

Before visiting Leticia, I had heard about the issue with child exploitation, but I had now been in the middle of it. The real stories I knew about the children I had personally met were tough to comprehend. I had walked by homes in the barrio where some of the kids had grown up as babies. No running water, no electricity, nothing more than plywood nailed together, making a box for a home.

Once, a girl who captured my heart began throwing up as she prayed with a lady, recounting the fear and instability that she had grown up with in her life. I could go on and on with these stories, no longer just tales that I read. These were real children, real situations that I'd seen before my very eyes.

We had to be involved. I had heard, but now I had seen. I knew this would begin a lifelong connection between the Harvey's and the orphanage. I didn't know how this would play out, but I would trust and obey.

The Fire Spreads

As the months went on, everyone around me, especially at Bellevue, heard about what was going on in Leticia, and we began raising an army to do great work. My kids led other kids in running a lemonade stand, where they raised money for orphans. It was great seeing my kids impacted.

Once, our Bible class completed a project to supply Bibles for the children. We all gathered as families one night, bought a Bible for each of the eighty children, and had their names engraved on them. Each family was designated a child and wrote letters to him or her, which they inserted into the child's Bible. We then packed the Bibles and sent them to Leticia. It was a great idea—except there was the small matter of shipping. I had heard never to ship something to Leticia, but after working with a friend in the logistics industry, I thought I had found a way. I had, but that way still took the box over three months to arrive in the jungle.

After I had taken a few more trips to Leticia, over the span of about one and a half years, I felt comfortable to lead groups from Bellevue. One of the teams I led, made up mostly of people from our Bible class, met the box of Bibles when we arrived in Leticia. We were able to have a ceremony during which we presented the Bibles and notes to the kids. What an unforgettable, joy-filled time.

I have fond memories of these trips. From being bitten by a monkey on the ear (true story), to holding a sloth, to fishing on the Amazon, I experienced some wild stuff. One of my favorite trips was one I took with Riley, leading a group of nine-year-olds and about five dads. We had a blast. Our kids experienced an incredible time of bonding with the kids from the orphanage. And, the kids at the orphanage felt so special that we would care enough about them to bring our own kids. I pray those kids will remember that trip forever.

In Leticia, I became good friends with the leader of a local hotel. He hires young people from Leticia and has created an environment that is able to overcome the many social and cultural obstacles in the city. As he states, "The hotel gives the children opportunity, room for growth, and hope." It is a great model for all organizations aiming to involve youth in business. This hotel became the place I stayed whenever I traveled to Leticia.

Eventually, one of my good friends began to help me lead the trips. He was one of the men in my Bible class. I trained him, encouraged him, and let him lead both on those trips and in our Bible class. He would prove to be a huge help in keeping these ministries going at Bellevue over the years. I am thankful for his love for God and his desire to lead. Always train someone up!

As time went on, I began to think that the Harvey's were being called to live in Leticia, and so did my wife. We used to pray about it, and eventually, I believed we were ready. Scared, but ready. God had written the orphanage on our hearts, and our thoughts and prayers continuously drew us closer to those kids.

I remember a surprise party that my wife threw for me on my fortieth birthday. When asked to speak, I spoke about how good God had been to me through my first forty years and said that I couldn't wait to see what happened in the next forty. I looked at Shannon, and in our minds, we thought we might be moving south.

Threads of the Season of Grace

I entered this third season feeling behind in life, a little on edge as I looked around at the lives of my friends. I left this season a new person with a new life and a new purpose. The season of grace forever changed my life.

The thread of perspective was a welcome addition to my tapestry. I had a new perspective on others, their journeys, their lives. I faced the deaths of friends, which helped me understand the brevity of life. And I gained a better perspective of God, how big he is. Perspective ultimately helped me be brave, fear nothing, and have active faith. This is one thread, however, that I must continually magnify to receive its full benefit.

My entrepreneurial spirit was birthed in this season. I developed a love for small business and creating things. I believe I always had the spark in me from my upbringing, but the fire was lit during this season.

Love became a thread at this time too. Not love like we tend to say in our culture when we really mean that we like things, but love as in "two become one." With this thread, selfishness is relinquished and you live for someone else. This thread gives life, new meaning to why you are here.

Perhaps the most powerful thread to be woven into my fabric during this season, though, was the thread of absolute truth. Absolute truth is gained from the Bible, so essentially, I became biblically literate during this season. I now know what the book says.

Although culture would say this thread is abrasive, it is anything but that. Absolute truth, which comes from the Bible, says that we are all the same, full of sin. At our core, we are all messed-up people trying to find our way. None is better than the other. The thread of absolute truth gave me a new worldview, a lens through which to view everything, and it became my anchor in rough seas.

All of these thoughts and threads woven together made me risk-averse. But I came to feel that the safe, comfortable bubble that I had created was not my destiny. God wanted more from me, the opposite of safety.

Interesting. I began this season looking for what I described as a safe, comfortable bubble. I ended the season wanting to bust the bubble and live a life going after God, anything but safe.

Reflect on your Season 3

For personal reflection, answer these questions about your journey.

- What are the 3 to 5 decisions that most impacted your life during this season?
- Who are the 5 people that had the biggest positive impact on your life?
- How did previous seasons impact season 3?
    - How did the beliefs on religion and God play out in season 3?
    - How did your view of people from previous seasons impact you in season 3?
    - How did the areas where you have lived impact your journey in season 3?
- What storms came into your life and describe the impact of these storms.
- What threads were developed?
- List evidence of God's grace in your life during this season.
- What was your anchor during this season?
- Looking over this season, what are 3 pieces of advice you give your family, friends, the world.

Name this season in your life.

For a detailed format to record your journey, check out the Seasons Journal.

Season 4:
The Wilderness

And behold, I am with you always, to the end of the age.

MATTHEW 28:20 (ESV)

The wilderness. A lonely place full of fear, with no direction to safety. A place where all hope vanishes. Nothing makes sense. You look for stability, a safety net, an anchor, but the world offers no peace. The wilderness causes panic, anxiety, and overwhelming thoughts. And, the wilderness comes swiftly.

You will not see the wilderness coming. If you did, you would change course. After all, we spend our lives doing everything to avoid the wilderness, don't we? We try to live the American dream—a nice, safe life free from danger and risk and surrounded by the comforts of our culture.

Consequently, our kids are raised in bubbles, an unfair picture of things to come. They grow and end up following culture, filing in, staying on the path. We inadvertently teach that the game of life is a game of striving for comfort and materialism. We inadvertently teach that life isn't about Jesus but about safety.

Because of our desire for comfort, we mold our beliefs into a different brand of Christianity. We create a different Jesus. A Jesus who desires our comfort in this world.

With this mindset, we are not mentally or spiritually prepared for the difficult times. The wilderness blindsides us, and we are shaken to the core. Only then do we look for an anchor. Only then do we tend to run to our Father.

A great example of this for me is what happened on 9/11. Our world was rocked. My world was rocked. When I showed up at church the following Sunday, we had to walk a mile to get in the building. Everyone was at church. At the most desperate point in their lives, in the wilderness, people sprinted to the church, as they were looking for solid ground.

Now, I am not saying we should not be running here. We should. We must run to Jesus when in the wilderness. I am, however, saying that we must not wait until the wilderness to run to the cross, as if Jesus is some type of genie to be called upon when we need wishes granted to get us out of hard times. We must prepare for the seasons of want now.

An absolute truth in this world is that you will find yourself in the wilderness. Wilderness will come to everyone. It may take the form of money. You may lose it all. Or maybe it will manifest as sickness or death, in which case money means nothing. Wilderness might even be mental battles of stress, depression, or loneliness. No one can say what wilderness you will face, but it will happen, so I encourage you to prepare.

The best way I know to prepare for the wilderness is to pick up your Bible. Become biblically literate. Understand who God really is, not who culture says he is. Don't shy away from the light that is found in God's Word, for this is the only light that will guide you in the darkness of the wilderness.

Thankfully, I knew God and his Word intimately when I stepped into the wilderness. To say I was fully prepared, though, would be a lie. At forty, my life was seemingly great. My family, my business, and my ministry were all blessed beyond belief. Everything I touched seemed to succeed. I think that I was fooled into thinking that there was no wilderness, not for me at least. I didn't realize I was headed there.

As you'll see, the wilderness came suddenly. I found myself looking around, second-guessing everything in my life. I had never been in a situation of having to lead my family when I did not know the path we would take. My wife and I were looking at an unknown future. Her faith was unwavering, but I must admit, I questioned mine. I heard Dr. Rogers say one time, "If you have never doubted your faith, then I doubt you are a Christian." Well, I can now check that box.

Even still, though, in the middle of it all, I knew that I was doubting something that was absolutely true. In fact, I would constantly tell myself that I did not want to look back at this period in my life and remember that I'd turned from my faith. I wanted to look at the wilderness and remember how I clung to God.

And I did cling to God. I had trouble praying, believing, and having faith, but I clung to my Father. Often this just looked like inwardly reciting what I knew Jesus said in Matthew 28:20: "I am with you always, to the very end of the age." Biblical literacy. I can't stress it enough. It was so important for me during the wilderness season when I had little else to work with. I thank God that he prepared me and gave me an anchor.

The Decision

Increasingly I felt the tug to leave my company for the sake of the orphanage in Leticia. I was knee-deep in reading my Bible, and nothing I read talked about living safely. Again I say, the Bible is not a "light read." It is not safe. It is not comfortable. Outside of God's sovereignty, there is nothing safe about following him. A life lived following God is a life of faith, trust, and adventure.

I began praying Romans 12:2: "Don't copy the behaviors and customs of this world, but let God transform you into a new person by changing the way you think. Then you will learn to know God's will for you, which is good and pleasing and perfect" (NLT). If I was, indeed, to leave my job, God would have to change the way I thought.

You never know when God will change the direction of your life. It can happen in an instant. He will guide you down a different path, where the two questions are "Am I listening?" and "Will I obey?" I felt I was ready, but you never know until God calls you.

I began talking to many people, including friends, pastors,

and business leaders, about what God was doing in my life. All, especially the business leaders, felt the residual impact of the economy's step back in 2008. The consistent message to me was not to take the risk of leaving my great career. I knew the Proverb that says, "In a multitude of counselors there is safety" (Prov. 24:6 NKJV), so I did not discount what they were saying. However, I also knew that I was following God, so that overrode the risk.

Once, I asked the president of a local seminary about risk from a biblical standpoint. I only remember that the question was not answered thoroughly but, from my perspective, danced around. I finally came to the conclusion that I would not talk to anyone else about what God was doing in my life. I felt that every human has a little world in them and I needed to sit at the feet of my Father. That is both a safe and dangerous place to be. Safe, because God is sovereign. Dangerous, because he is not interested in your worldly comfort.

A truth observed throughout the Bible is that God speaks. We see it everywhere from his speaking the world into existence to his sending his Son to earth to his commanding rough seas to still. God always speaks. He speaks through his Word, through prayer, and through people. The question is, does humanity listen?

One morning as I was studying the Bible at our house in Germantown, I wrote down in my journal the reasons I could not leave the company that had blessed me and my family. I listed great reasons, like my 401(k), college for my kids, retirement, and our house. The list felt so me-absorbed. I began praying Romans 12:2, and I sensed God asking me to write down every promise that he had ever given me. I started writing every verse that he'd given me, and I ended up writing three pages of promises.

I then began crossing through everything that I had written on my list of reasons I could not leave. My 401(k)? God had it. College for my kids? God had it. Retirement? God had it. Our house and material possessions? God had it. I surrendered all to Jesus that morning. I was going to completely depend on him. I listened. I was to leave my job, devote myself to the orphanage, and depend on the furniture business for my well-being. Better said, I was to depend on God for my well-being.

It has always been hard for me to articulate the events of that morning in a manner that one fully comprehends. God's call on your life is unique, individual to you. You can't accurately put into words the moment that call comes. You can only know in yourself that God spoke, God called. That is enough to propel you into action.

So, I sheepishly walked upstairs to report to my wife what had happened. She was reading her Bible as I talked through the message I believed to be from God, that I was to leave my job. Her exact words as she looked me dead in the eyes: "I was wondering when you were going to say that. I know that is what you're supposed to do."

That settled it. I would never have made the decision to leave my job if Shannon did not agree 100 percent. This was not my decision, but our decision.

Departure

O ver the next few weeks, a lot changed. The manager of my business, the key to its success over the last six years, told me of his desire to leave the business. He had an opportunity to work for a growing company in Mississippi.

The news was a surprise to me, but this certainly could help the financials of the business. He would be greatly missed, but I had a strong, capable assistant manager at the store who could manage the day-to-day operations of the business. I felt this could work. I could focus on the orphanage, and he could focus on the business. I would provide strategic oversight, and he would handle the tactics.

Next up, I formally communicated my decision to my boss. His reaction? Complete shock. After some initial back-and-forth about what he could do to convince me to stay, the discussion ended. He realized that this was about something bigger, a passion that this company couldn't quench.

After telling him the news, I went back to my office to digest what had just happened. I was relieved that I'd told him but scared to death about taking the next step. In the middle of this, my boss came into my office. "How does one get faith like you?" he asked. I told him how I didn't have great faith, that he shouldn't put me on a pedestal, and I talked to him about Jesus.

Within the next week or so, we had a conference call with the broader team to announce my departure. After I shared the news, you could have heard a pin drop. The quietness was frightening to me. This move was really happening. The news penetrated the team, convicted some and led others to believe I was crazy, but all respected my decision. The job had come to an end.

To help you understand my mindset, following is a blog post that I typed during this time, in April 2011, when I was forty-two:

All Because I Said Yes, April 2011
   From a "Christian life" to a life of faith and obedience. From the "American dream" to a mission of "connecting kids, feeding poor children, and assisting in lifting communities out of poverty."
   All because I said "yes" to God's will for my life.
   I was living a safe, Christian life. I went to church, read the Bible, prayed, and tried to live a "good" life. I have discovered through reading the Bible that if this was how I defined my Christian life, I was missing it. My life simply did not stack up to what I read in the Bible. As I read and God spoke, I faced an unavoidable collision with my safe, "Christian" life. After all, there is only one way to interpret Jesus's command to feed the poor. God consistently showed me his character of caring for the poor and the orphans. God clearly directed me to do something in my life to address these issues. God has a plan for each of our lives, and this is his personal plan for me.
   As my faith has grown, God has given me the confidence to step out for him. My faith is not about my denomination. It is not about whether an individual is sprinkled or baptized. It is not about whether you live a "good" life or not. I believe the Bible. That's it. I believe that Jesus Christ was the Son of God. I believe that we can each have a personal relationship with him and he will change your life. That is my faith. Pretty simple.
   This blog will serve as a way to follow my work as I partner to accomplish a mission set forth by God to "connect kids, feed poor

children, and assist in lifting communities out of poverty."
I covet your prayers for me and my family.

I immediately went to work on the vision to "connect kids, feed poor children, and assist in lifting communities out of poverty." My number one goal was to figure out a way to make the orphanage sustainable. I knew that the model of making trips back to the United States to ask for support, especially in a down economy, may not last. I wanted to figure out a new way, and the concept of microfinance captivated me.

A man on a mission, I read, studied, and went to every conference I could that had to do with microfinance. Through my research, I heard of an orphanage in Chile that had started businesses whose proceeds were used to run the home. The orphanage had started about fifteen small businesses, like a t-shirt company, which provided them with a sustainable source of income as well as a way to teach the kids business. This model made a lot of sense to me. I thought it was perfect for our situation, so I began to figure out how to make it happen.

The most obvious obstacle before me was that I lacked experience. I had a vision, a passion, and a familiarity with Colombia, but I did not have the expertise needed to get the mission off the ground. I needed help creating these small businesses. In various conversations, I heard of an expert on the subject who had started businesses for the poor all over the world. He had even written a book on the subject. I read his book, called him, and shared my vision with him. I explained that I lacked the knowledge to carry out the mission and asked if he would work as a consultant on the project. We worked out the details, and he was in.

Shortly following, I held a small meeting at a local hotel conference room in Germantown with leaders in and around Memphis. I flew in our new consultant to the meeting, we talked about the future of the orphanage, and I presented the vision to all in attendance. This group incited great energy and enthusiasm around the launch of our work to make the home sustainable. Our meeting ended with the plan that I would create a prospectus to present for financial backing of the project.

I gave the project a name: the Leticia Economic Development Project (LEDP). I then created an LEDP advisory board and began circulating the LEDP prospectus. Following is a blog post that I wrote in mid-2011, highlighting my vision:

> *Everyone,*
>
> *Let me start of by apologizing (again). My last update was 3 months ago. At this point, I will not promise to update regularly.*
>
> *Quite a bit has evolved since my last update.*
>
> *I continue to work on a mission to connect kids, feed poor children, and assist in lifting communities out of poverty.*
>
> *I just returned from an incredible trip to Colombia. After months of planning, we officially kicked off the Leticia Economic Development Project (LEDP) in-country.*
>
> *The mission statement of the LEDP is to develop a sustainable, self-funding solution for the orphanage through economic development.*
>
> *We had an expert in the field of international business travel with us on the trip in a consulting role. He has worked on economic development projects for the poor around the world, most recently in Haiti. Interestingly, he and his wife have lived in Northern Colombia for 2 years where they started ADIN, Asociación para el Desarrollo Integral, creating hundreds of businesses and jobs.*
>
> *He and I spent our time planting the vision with individuals around Leticia. We met with government agencies, business owners, and young entrepreneurs. As a result of our meetings, we were able to lay the foundation for the project. Five extremely talented Colombia businesspeople passionately accepted our LEDP board invitation. These non-salaried positions are responsible for the following.*
>
> - *Hire the project director*
>
> - *Hold initial weekly meetings with director to discuss business opportunities*
>
> - *Agreement on 2 to 5 businesses to pursue*
>
> - *Review and approve business plans presented by the director*

- *Review the plans with the team for funding consideration*

Since our return, the board has met twice, elected the officers, and began to pursue businesses. One of the original board members was elected as project director, a salaried position with the following responsibilities.

- *Participate in weekly board meetings*

- *Agreement on 2 to 5 businesses to pursue*

- *Develop business plans for each business, including capital needed*

- *Hire managers for businesses (if needed); director may manage business*

- *Present businesses to board*

The LEDP is underway, we have the board in place, the project director has been hired, and the group is actively pursuing businesses. Some of the businesses currently being pursued are construction projects, a bakery, exporting fish, and chicken farming.

As I began my week in Colombia, I was very over-whelmed. I was 2,500 miles from home, didn't speak the language, and trying to start businesses. As I finished my trip, without a shadow of a doubt, I can say that God is good.

I wait with great anticipation to see what he will do with our work in Colombia.

Wow. I read that blog and I am blown away when I think about what God was doing during that time. We had a seemingly solid plan, great passion, great people, and great momentum. We were ready to take on the project.

Over the next six months, we began to dig our heels into the LEDP process that we had created, analyzing businesses including a tilapia fish farm, a deli, a donut shop, a taxi service, and an Amazonian herb farm. Additionally, we held meetings with local business owners. We taught them simple foundational business skills and financial acumen.

As we researched the area, we found that the number one industry was the travel and tourism industry. People came from all around to travel the Amazon River, porting in Leticia. With this came an influx of people in the downtown area, which was full of markets and shops. This industry seemed like our best shot at getting a business going.

We worked extensively with a man who lived in the barrio on the edge of the Amazon jungle. He was an incredible craftsman who created art by hand from "blood wood," a hardwood found in the Amazon. A single father, having lost his wife early in life to disease, he didn't have sufficient income to care for his kids' needs and therefore relied on the orphanage to provide for them full-time.

One day, I visited his shop. His shop, which was really just an open area in the jungle behind his house, was located in the middle of the barrio, where all the houses were shacks built of four plywood sheets. During this visit, I asked him what his dreams were concerning his work, his business. His reply surprised me. He told me that he was living his dream, that his business couldn't be any better. After all, he was the wealthiest man in the barrio. Life was great. There was no thought of having his kids move back in with him or moving out of the barrio. The barrio was his home. I learned a few valuable lessons from this discussion, and I was left with burning questions.

The first lesson I learned: poverty creates a glass ceiling—a life surrounded by imaginary walls that never allow you to see the opportunity that exists beyond. In the West, we see opportunities in business and in life. We believe that we can. But poverty causes you to believe that you can't. You are where you are. How do you change the perception created by a life of poverty?

Secondly, I understood better that a radically different view of wealth exists in the West. I came from a life of materiality, where I had more than I would ever need. The business owner felt the same way about his situation. He had all that he'd ever needed. As he said, "Look around the village. I am the wealthiest here." His measure was against his peers in extreme poverty. He never recognized his ability to rise above the village, out of poverty. He was content, and he quite possibly had the better view of wealth. Was my perception of needs misguided because of where I lived?

Lastly, poverty de-emphasized his role as the leader of a family, the person responsible for his children. This business owner was living for himself. His children were the responsibility of society in his mind, and thus the orphanage entered the picture. This was a situation when helping actually hurt. (There is a great book on this topic by a similar name, by the way.) Were we enabling his behavior by caring for his kids?

Honestly, this was tough. For the first time, I began to ask myself, how you help people who have a different, and maybe more accurate, view of the world than you? My answer was money, generate wealth. This was the key to helping.

With this thought in mind, we ended up funding that man's business and flying him to Bogota to a craft fair in a city of fifteen million people. This was a remarkable trip for him, but still, even after the experience, he was content in his village. I thought I had found the perfect business to test the LEPD, to better a man's life, and to help the orphanage that cared for his kids; however, he saw no need to grow the business. By his standards, he was just fine. Maybe he was right.

The answer for the man ultimately had to be the gospel. The answer was not more income, a flourishing business, or a new home. God had absolute truth that could transform his mind, give the man hope and eternal life. We could not force beliefs or a change in action. I was reminded of how God was in control, had to be in control.

A Change in Direction

Our orphanage in Leticia leased a great facility. In it, we were able to house about thirty kids permanently and care for an additional forty each day. We did have plans to build a new facility to house more children, as the need was great, but we were on our timeline.

As we were knee-deep in researching businesses, out of nowhere, the timeline shifted. We received a letter from the owners of the building saying that we would be removed from the leased facility. A national church denomination owned the building and wanted to plant a church. Yes, they wanted to remove the orphanage to plant a church. God was in control, but this bothered me. I was reminded of what the Bible calls pure and genuine religion: caring for orphans.

Obviously, our focus changed a bit. We no longer had time to invest and grow businesses to create a revenue stream. We had to quickly find a facility. We looked and looked for a building that would work. There were a few potentials, but the owners were very proud of their land. One would think property would be cheap in Leticia, but the city is waterlocked, hemmed in by the Amazon jungle and the river. There was not much open land to build on. The owners knew the situation and wanted to capitalize.

One day, a pastor contacted the head of the orphanage. He knew of eight acres that were for sale by a local church member. When we checked out the land, we found it to be in a perfect location, near the church with which we had a partnership. Additionally, the land was near an airport where international teams could easily travel in and out. As we prayed and researched the land, a board member stepped up to purchase the plot. We now had a course set for the future home of the orphanage.

Shortly after the purchase, we had plans for a beautiful new home drawn by an architect. The future orphanage would have more space to house kids, a retail store with local handmade goods to help fund monthly expenses, and classroom space for community training events. We put together a capital campaign and begin sharing the mission.

The development of the land hit roadblock after roadblock. From areas of the parcel that flooded in the rainy season to lack of qualified help to clear the land, we felt that we were never going to break ground on a facility. Discouragement was beginning to set in, and we were asking God if this was really what we were to do.

When we began this journey, our guiding Bible verse was Psalm 127:1: "Unless the Lord builds the house, the builders labor in vain." At times, I felt we were laboring in vain, and I would return to this verse in prayer. He was in control.

Many years earlier, the director of the orphanage had met a guy who led a nonprofit organization in Switzerland that built schools for the poor around the world. Well, one day, as God would have it, this man from Switzerland contacted her to see if she had any needs. Within a few months, the organization was in Leticia, at last breaking ground on the site of the new orphanage. Amazing! Although the structure and design were not what we originally had in mind, it was exactly how God had planned it. It was perfect. God had again moved before our very eyes. We did nothing; he made it happen.

In spite of the change in plans, my journey with the orphanage and Colombia continued to progress. Things were going great. My faith continued to grow as I recognized even more that God was in control.

Failure

Back at my small business, I couldn't get the momentum going. My focus had been in Colombia, and frankly, I had not been the leader I needed to be. I had spent no time on strategic vision for the company and completely left the business mentally.

Sales began to falter, and I found myself spending more and more time trying to keep it going. We started putting more of a holistic marketing program together, including TV, radio, billboards, and various local sponsorships, such as one with the Memphis Redbirds, a Minor League Baseball team.

The more I dug into the business, the more areas of concern I discovered. The business needed a lot of attention, and I could not generate sustainable sales with my minimal efforts. More importantly, I had very little passion left for the business. My passion was in Colombia.

I felt that with the right people leading, the right focus, the business could again flourish. However, it was clear: I was not the right person. So, working with a business broker, I put the business for sale.

This was a monumental decision for the Harvey's. Remember, I had felt that God had led me to utilize the business to fund the home. While the business generated profits, I was to focus my time on the sustainability efforts of the orphanage. Before making the decision to leave my career for this task, I had prayed, researched, and thought continuously about it. I felt that I had "counted the costs."

And it wasn't just me. My wife and I were in this together. We'd both thought we were looking at a move to Colombia in our near future. Shannon had prepared our lives and minds for us to become missionaries in Leticia. You could have asked us any day if we were ready, and we would have said, "Absolutely."

Yet now, things had changed. This piece of the journey had not been considered. A business failure, a mission failure, a vision failure. I say a mission and vision failure because I had not succeeded in making the orphanage sustainable. My dream had not been fulfilled. I couldn't help but wonder if I had missed God's voice in my life, if I had missed his direction.

This situation began a dark period in my life, probably the darkest. I was not only funding some of the work in Leticia but also a floundering business. I felt my journey had ended.

Darkness

I'd started the journey invigorated, excited to see what God was going to do. However, as the business receded along with my personal funds, I was down and my faith was waning. I could no longer focus on the orphanage, leading the Bible fellowship class, or my family.

During this time, I remember attempting to pray at the business but literally having no words. I didn't know what to say. I just cried. Matthew 28:20 immediately came to mind: "I am with you always, to the very end of the age." I knew that was all I needed. Jesus. He was with me, and that had to be enough.

But I was so empty that at one point, I picked up my Bible, turned to Shannon, and asked, "Is there anything to what I have been reading and following?"

As only Shannon could, she turned to me and said, "Would you please shut up and start being the spiritual leader of this home?" Ouch. She was right.

I went on a long jog that day. For me, running is a way to settle my soul, my faith, my mind. I had a special place where I jogged in Memphis, through the woods, next to Wolf River in Germantown and East Memphis. Those woods are a sacred place for me. Over the years, I spent a lot of time on my knees there, crying to God. And on this run in the woods, I discovered what I needed to do.

With the business for sale, I decided to step away from the work in Leticia. Imagine, walking away from this amazing ministry. It didn't make sense, but we had to leave this part of the journey. Shannon and I thought, prayed, and looked at the landscape, and we both felt God was no longer calling us to Colombia.

God had raised up a dynamic ministry to support the orphanage, so this gave us great comfort. However, there will always be a burning question this side of heaven if the Harvey's were supposed to move to Colombia. With all of our heart, Shannon and I didn't believe this to be the case, but we wonder. There will always, too, be a hole in my heart for the orphanage and the city. As I type this, I long to be more involved in the ministry.

Everything seemed to be falling apart. My plan had not come to pass as I had hoped. At one time, the path was clear; everything was easy to see. Now, no clarity existed and the path was dark. This was exactly where God wanted me, though. Depending on him.

Shannon and I were ready for the new chapter of our lives, but we had no clue what that meant. We still had the weight of the business, so we were praying for a sale. I began throwing my name in the hat for different jobs. With my background, we both knew that we could end up moving to the Northwest Arkansas area. We didn't like the thought of this, but Memphis didn't have a lot of companies that made sense for me.

One of my first calls was to a friend I had previously worked with who was now living in Northwest Arkansas. He told me of another friend of his who he felt had a similar heartbeat to mine and had started a business. My friend wasn't sure exactly what the company was all about or if they were hiring, but he encouraged me to look them up.

I read what I could about the company and called his friend.

I don't remember much about that conversation, but I do remember that I loved the vision for the company. The company existed to glorify God by doing what I knew how to do, manage retail businesses. The conversation was just an introduction, though, not an interview. He said that he would keep my name in mind as business needs came up.

My search intensified. I contacted numerous companies and placement agencies. One opportunity that came my way was with a technology company, managing a portion of the business. The job came down to myself and one other person. We both flew to San Francisco for our final interviews. I couldn't have been more prepared. I presented a strategy document I had drafted in advance and left feeling the interviews went great. I was excited.

As I was waiting on word from this company, I drove to Arkansas for an interview with a different company. This interview seemed to be a dead end, and I drove back to Memphis optimistically waiting for the call with the job offer from the technology company.

It was a rainy evening. I was driving down I-40 between Little Rock and Northwest Arkansas when I received the call. I didn't get the job. Honestly, I was shaken, discouraged, bewildered. I called Shannon and shared the news, and I just had this burning feeling that she was losing confidence in me. It wasn't true, but I feared it was.

On this stretch of road, I looked up and noticed a huge cross on a hill that I had never noticed before. What a gift at that moment. Whoever put that cross there has no idea how they spoke to me that night. I didn't see God's leading at the time, but I knew I did not want to look back and see that I had left him during this dark period in my life. I wanted to look back and see that I'd depended on him, clung to him. And so, I did, desperately. I was confused, but looking at that cross, I acknowledged he was in control, and that gave me great peace. Within three years of my interview, that technology company, a large, growing company, would be out of business. God protected.

I ended up talking to another individual about a job opportunity for which I could be based in Memphis. What a godsend! I would manage the east half of the US, work from home, and earn a great salary. It was an ideal opportunity. I interviewed a few times and was about to receive the offer. Shannon and I were pumped that we would not be leaving Memphis. Our friends were here, our church was here, our family was near. We had deep roots that we would not have to dig up.

At about this same time, the friend of a friend I previously spoke to called and asked me to drive to Northwest Arkansas to meet a few people from his company. No harm could be done, so, with the Memphis job seemingly safely in hand, I drove to Arkansas. I had an awesome visit meeting the partners and some leadership. This company was definitely a place I wanted to work, but they were small. Things had shifted in the business, and they didn't have any immediate openings.

God seemed to be leading the Harvey's to remain in Memphis. However, for some reason, the job offer for the Memphis opportunity was delayed. They called me, assuring me that this would come to fruition and the offer was just hung up internally.

A few weeks went by. No offer. Meanwhile, the company in Arkansas called again and asked if I could come up, as they had an opportunity for which they thought I would be a good fit. I had a couple of interviews, and the job was, indeed, a great fit in an area where my experience existed. In fact, I don't think it could have been a more perfect fit.

So, a couple of opportunities now seemed realistic. I liked the company in Arkansas, especially since I had ties to some people there, but the job in Memphis seemed to be much better for our family. We all really wanted to stay in Memphis. We continued to wait for that offer to come in.

Meanwhile, we had a family vacation to Seacrest Beach, Florida planned, our normal getaway. We couldn't wait. We needed a break. On the drive down, I received a call from the company in Memphis with the job offer. I pulled over and got out of the car so I could focus on the conversation. This was the opportunity that my family and I had been waiting for, my next move. The financials of the job exceeded expectations, the challenge of managing the eastern half of the US would be great, and I would start when I returned.

The best news about this offer was that now my family would remain in Memphis. Memphis was where Shannon and I met, where we were married, where our kids were born, where our church was, where our kids were dedicated, where Riley and Natalie accepted Jesus, and where our deep, deep friendships were. Memphis was passionately our place, our people. Our people meant so much to us, more than family. We had grown up in marriage together, wept together, led others to Christ together, prayed together, raised kids together, leaned on each other, and generally done life together. What a blessing this job opportunity was for us.

Shannon wept when I told her the news as I was getting back in the car. We told the kids, and the celebration began. We arrived in Florida ready to relax, hit the beach, and enjoy the week. However, things changed quickly.

Shortly after unloading the car, we were at the pool and I received a call. The company in Arkansas was calling to tell me they had an offer for me. Honestly, I didn't feel that it would be competitive with the other offer, and this would prove to be true. Besides, we were already emotionally remaining in Memphis. The Harvey's were good. Nonetheless, I loved the company culture and what they were about, so I listened. After hearing the offer, I told them how much I appreciated it but said this just was not the right timing for our family. I ended the conversation with great peace. Off to the beach!

I sent the following email to my Arkansas friends that evening:

Over the last year and a half, my wife and I have been through radical changes. We left corporate America to do mission work with the orphanage in Colombia. This has been more of a blessing than I could ever imagine, but it has also been more of a challenge than I could ever imagine. The challenge has mainly been from a financial perspective, as we have been under a lot of stress that a volunteer, non-pay position brings. We were completely aware of this challenge and accepted God's will to do this work, so we do praise Him for what he has brought us through and taught us. In fact, we would not change a thing.

As I step back and look at my next move, I have to consider what my family has been through over the last year and a half. As the spiritual leader, if given the opportunity, I need to lead my family to a season of peace, mainly from a financial perspective. At this point, we simply can't endure another season of stress in this area of our lives.

As I reviewed the package, I realized that the offer delivered will not give us a season of relief. The monthly financial stress, combined with the moving expense, will not alleviate the pressure we have felt over the last year. All the things that come with a new home, combined with the financial pressure, would put my family in a very difficult situation.

As you know, last Thursday, I received another offer. This offer will provide our family with a season of financial peace. The financial package is too big of a difference for me to choose the company. If I was leaving my original position, I would jump at the chance to work for the company, happily taking a step backwards in pay. However, with the season my family is leaving, I must choose differently.

I write this email with a heavy heart as, simply put, I would love to work for the company. I believe in your vision, and I can see myself as part of the team. In fact, the company vision lines up perfectly with my personal life mission statement. However, as the spiritual leader of my family, at this time, I just can't make the numbers work. This might not be God's timing for either one of us, and I know that I speak for both of us in saying that His will is best.

Know that I really enjoyed getting to know the company and pray that God blesses your efforts. I will be talking to the other company Monday around noon. I will call the office tomorrow morning.

Sincerely,

Mike

James 1:27 - Pure and genuine religion in the face of God the Father means caring for orphans and widows in their distress and refusing to let the world corrupt you.

The next day, prior to sending the acceptance email to the Memphis company, I received a call from the company in Arkansas, and in a matter of a few hours, I had a new offer. An offer that didn't compare to the Memphis one from a worldly standpoint, but an offer that seemed to have my heart.

My heart was torn over the two different paths that I could lead my family down. On the one hand, we could remain in Memphis, close to family, friends, relationships, and church with little change to our life. The other path, though, offered an opportunity to work for a company with a mission similar to my life's mission. I talked to my wife, and she was torn as well. She would support either direction.

The next morning, I arose early to begin my day like I did

all others. I headed to the beach at about 5:00 a.m. with my Bible in hand. As I read, I wept and talked to my Father about the future, about both job opportunities. It was clear what he wanted me to do. Although I knew the difficulty of the decision, I had to go to Arkansas. I looked down to grab a stone of remembrance, a seashell that I have to this day, and headed back to our house.

As soon as my wife walked in the kitchen, I told her the news. She looked down. Then, the most spiritually wise person in my life, she said through tears, "I know." We hugged, cried, and rejoiced that God was leading. Deep down, there was great excitement about this new venture.

Now, the hard part. We had to tell our kids we were leaving Memphis. We went to the beach that morning, and I gathered the family together. As I shared the news, Riley, nine years old at the time, broke down crying. She did not want to leave Memphis. Natalie and Griffin quickly followed suit. What a great way for Dad to kick off the vacation! We spent some time together on the beach after that, mentally preparing for the journey to come.

It was settled. We were moving. The acceptance email that I was about to send to the other company was never sent.

Goodbye, Memphis

Our friends in Memphis, knowing what the Harvey's had been through, leaned in to help us with the move. They joined us in prayer and were available whenever we needed help.

Many times when going through difficult things, well-meaning people will ask how they can pray for you. Our friends, though, just jumped in and made things happen. For example, some of our close friends saw a need in our house and stepped forward to give us new hardwood for our dining room as we prepared the home for sale. We have countless stories of our community's helping us, which demonstrates why it was so difficult to leave.

We had two big needs to make the move successful: the selling of a house and the selling of a business. Both seemed unlikely, as I would be starting with my new company in about four weeks. Well, God showed up.

A couple who owned another business in Germantown showed great interest in our business. They had been inquiring about the business for a few months, but no offers had materialized. It was a natural fit for them, as they had the expertise to grow the business. I felt they would be the perfect owners.

As God would have it, they were the perfect owners. They were passionately, emotionally drawn to our business and had a vision of what it could become. After working through a lot of details, they bought the business. The sale was a great blessing to our family. There was no way I could have operated the business from Arkansas. It would have been a huge burden to deal with during the move.

I came to know the new owners personally, and I hoped that they would be blessed by the business. However, over the course of a year, this was not the case. The business only lasted an additional eighteen months or so before the new owners closed the doors to focus on their other business.

Concerning our house, I knew we would lose money on the sale. The housing market in Germantown had not recovered after the downturn in the economy. I was not worried about losing money, though; I just needed a reasonable offer.

While we were trying to sell the house, I started work, driving back and forth between Memphis and the office in Arkansas. I was employee twenty-three, and I was excited to be part of the journey of a company that sought to glorify God.

I traveled back and forth for about four weeks, keeping track of the Germantown house showings with Shannon. Within a few weeks, we received a reasonable offer on our home. Shannon and I immediately accepted, knowing that we needed to get the family back together in Arkansas.

Threads from the Wilderness Season

As I reflect on the last chapter of our life in Memphis, I realize that I have severely understated the challenge it presented to me as a husband, father, and leader of my family.

My personal battle was in an area that would have been unknown had it not been for the gift of the wilderness. Yes, the wilderness was a gift. Because the center of the struggle in the wilderness was where I found my self-worth. It would have remained dormant forever had God not interceded and led us through this season.

Prior to this time, I inadvertently tied my self-worth to professional equity and the wealth that I created. My career, my status, my money defined me. People knew me as a successful businessperson, and I craved this admiration. I depended on my career and my wealth for my happiness.

Wealth is the great blind spot, especially in the United States. Maybe that is why Jesus talked more about money than any other subject. The Bible doesn't say that money is the root of all evil but that the love of money is the root of all evil (1 Tim. 6:10). One may claim that Jesus is number one in their life, that they depend on him for all, that they have great faith, but I don't believe that you ever realize your dependence on wealth and your career until it is ripped away. After all, why do you need faith when you have all the material wealth that you will ever need?

If you don't think you are wealthy, it's possible you need to reevaluate. Compared to the majority of the world that lives on four dollars a day, most of us in the United States are ridiculously wealthy.

I have a spiritual mentor who lives in the Amazon jungle running an orphanage. She lives on about five hundred dollars a month, constantly going without to provide for the kids.

This meek warrior in a small body tells many stories of how God showed up when all hope was lost. She is 100 percent dependent on her God to care for her and provide for her. He is enough. Her self-worth is found in her Lord. I have never seen dependence on God like from this mentor of mine. Her faith is extreme. It makes me uncomfortable and convicts me to my core. I want this faith.

So to me, the thread, the gift, given to me during the wilderness was new vision, the ability to see the indirect correlation between wealth and faith. As wealth increases, faith decreases. It has to, as you don't need anything. And as wealth decreases, faith increases. It has to, because you are forced to depend on God. I try to magnify this new vision thread in my tapestry.

For all those out there who are saying, "If I can just make a little more money" or "If I can just move into this position, then I will be content," beware. The price paid could be your faith. I know that this is hard to believe, because we are lulled into thinking pridefully that our faith is great, our dependence on God is great. That is exactly why the dependence on wealth is a blind spot.

A great test is what the traveling minister Manley Beasley would always say: what are you depending on right now that would leave you sunk if it went away? Most often, the answer is money. It was for me, until the wilderness removed the scales from my eyes.

Indeed, leaving my job to focus on the work in Colombia, from an earthly standpoint, was a horrible career and financial move. I thought I had counted the costs, but I had no idea. I lost a whole lot of money, and I lost a whole lot of professional equity. I essentially started over on both. Everything that I valued on earth from a professional standpoint was gone.

I question a lot, did I really recognize God's will for my life when I left my job for Colombia? Was this decision emotionally driven? Did I miss it? Here's the deal. Outside of the direct truths in God's Word, I am never 100 percent sure of his will. I can talk myself out of things. I can pray myself out of things. So, if I think that God is calling me to do something and I am over 50 percent confident that he is indeed calling, I will go. I have to go. That is faith. That is obedience. The outcome of the journey is in God's hands, and from reading Scripture, I know that it is never easy. In fact, it cost the people in the Bible a lot, and, it cost me a lot too. That is okay. I obey knowing that his ways are not my ways. I am thankful that God gave me faith to trust.

I also battle the thought of what my life would look like if I had not left my career. Honestly, I would be nearing an early retirement, as I had done a tremendous job of saving. Culture constantly presses into me with this thought.

For example, I was recently having dinner with a couple of God-fearing men. I recounted the story to them, and one of them said, in a sarcastic tone, "How did that decision work out for you?" Seriously, brother?

I still battle these thoughts and other falsehoods, and I must regularly give them to God. I imagine that I will battle these thoughts forever.

God is my rock, my Redeemer, my anchor. He is my hope. I depend on him. I believe that is why he put me on the journey that he did. He wanted me to depend on him more. I pray that I decrease and he increases (John 3:30).

I am thankful for a God who cares for his children like he does.

Reflect on your Season 4

For personal reflection, answer these questions about your journey.

- What are the 3 to 5 decisions that most impacted your life during this season?
- Who are the 5 people that had the biggest positive impact on your life?
- How did previous seasons impact season 4?
  - How did the beliefs on religion and God play out in season 4?
  - How did your view of people from previous seasons impact you in season 4?
  - How did the areas where you have lived impact your journey in season 4?
- What storms came into your life and describe the impact of these storms.
- What threads were developed?
- List evidence of God's grace in your life during this season.
- What was your anchor during this season?
- Looking over this season, what are 3 pieces of advice you give your family, friends, the world.

Name this season in your life.

For a detailed format to record your journey, check out the Seasons Journal.

Season 5: Renewal

I had heard of you by the hearing of the ear,
but now my eye sees you;

Renewal. On this stretch of the journey, the wilderness is quickly forgotten and optimism rules the day. Life is met with a feeling of invigoration and bullishness. A chance to start over.

The renewal season, indeed, is sweet. For me, this season of life was full of hope, excitement, and happiness. As the leader of my family, emerging from the wilderness, I had direction and strategy before me. This felt good.

As for my wife, she was being a faithful partner, obedient to her husband, but ultimately, Shannon just wanted to follow God. If he was leading, she wanted to file in.

Our kids were young and resilient. They were good with the move and would soon forget our lives in Memphis. Northwest Arkansas would be their home.

This is not to say, though, that the season of renewal is an easy one. Life would never be the same for my family. When I made the decision to leave my job in Memphis to focus on Colombia, ships were burned. We had to begin a new journey into uncharted waters.

The joy of leaving Memphis was that God had provided and we were following him. We would be leaving the wilderness to a place uniquely planned for us. Shannon and I knew this deep in our hearts, so our faith brought us comfort.

However, the pain was ever-present. We had lived in Memphis fifteen years around our church, our friends, our ministry, our business, our families, everything that we seemingly cared about. We loved Memphis, and our roots were deep in this city.

More than anything, though, the thought of leaving our friends hurt, and it especially hurt Shannon. As I've said, we had deep friendships that were like family relationships. There is a depth of relationship that develops between families when you go through different stages together, like marriage, the birth and growth of children, and the deepening of faith. A bond is formed that will never be taken away. This bond is to be cherished. It is a gift of God.

But, following God is greater than the things of this world.

It must be. The world is not our home. Although Shannon and I had read this truth many times in the Bible, we were now being taught what it meant. God was refining us, and refining is never fun or easy, but it is good.

The New Song

As we pulled out of our driveway, Griffin and I in one car and the girls behind us in the van, I looked in the rear-view mirror and saw three girls crying. I told Griffin that this would either be the best move that Dad had made or the worst. One thing for sure: life would no longer be the same.

Arriving in Northwest Arkansas was exciting. The area was growing rapidly and seemed to have two distinct cultures within thirty miles of each other. In the southernmost parts, you had the vibrant college town surrounding the University of Arkansas. To the north, the area was somewhat of a melting pot with people moving in from all over the world for the business opportunities that existed. The south had character created by the university; the north had character driven by the population growth.

Arkansas turned out to be more challenging than either Shannon or I ever imagined, mostly because of our deep love for Memphis. Our church, our community, the Memphis culture—this was the life we knew. So, unfortunately, we compared everything in Arkansas to what we had known in

Memphis. However, as we now say, we are lucky enough to have lived the life we had in Memphis, to have something with which to compare.

Northwest Arkansas was different, a truly new culture. Friends already had friends, and we found it difficult to break into circles. Many nights I came home from work and found Shannon crying, desperately trying to deal with the loss of her close circle of friends and her church, with her loneliness. The first year, the kids were homeschooled, which I think added to the loneliness. Shannon and the kids were not involved in school activities, logical avenues to build relationships.

I was lonely as well, but I had an office full of people to interact with daily. For me, any loneliness that I felt was drowned out by the fact that I had a new career I was engulfed in. I was driven by the need to be successful, to reestablish my career. I went into the move throwing my whole self at my job. For the good of my future, my family, I had to be all-in. Work had to be first. I never would have described it in such terms, but this was reality. So, lonely I was, but my mission overrode these feelings.

The one place that Shannon and I thought we would immediately build deep relationships was church. Having spent so long in our environment at Bellevue, we craved a tight biblical community. We thought this existed everywhere, in all churches. We found out that was not the case, though. The churches around us in Arkansas were different. So different, in fact, that we felt we did not belong. We struggled and wandered, not knowing where to join. Seemingly, the biblical community we'd been a part of had vanished; it was not present here. Shannon and I were doing a lot of soul-searching to figure out why.

We pointed to a couple of things that caused our struggle with church. First, church to the Harvey's was a place where community was to be found. At Bellevue, we had been at a stage of life that naturally created this community. We began there as a newly married couple spending time with a group of other newly married couples, all experiencing new things, trying to figure out how to build a marriage and family. It is logical that we grew close to these people, did life with this people, and built a community. In Arkansas, we entered church at a different life stage with kids at different ages, which made the experience radically different.

Second, I point to the fact that we "grew up" spiritually at Bellevue. I considered Adrian Rogers my mentor. Shannon and I learned so much about God and the Bible from him and the other church leaders at Bellevue. Shannon and I were married at Bellevue. Riley was baptized at Bellevue. We taught young married couples at Bellevue for many years. That church was truly home to us.

For those two reasons, church would always be different for Shannon and me. Not better, and not worse, just different. Looking back, we now know how unfair it was to compare the churches, to somehow put one on a pedestal over the others. God works differently in different churches. No two are the same.

Throughout this period, we uniquely learned that God is sovereign, and he continued to lead the Harvey's. Our dependence had to be on him, not on money, as I had already established, and neither on relationships built at church.

As the search for a church continued, Shannon and I were also wondering how we would continue to be involved with our Colombia ministry. One Sunday, we visited a church and ended up meeting the missions pastor. I asked him what was happening in missions at the church, and he told me about projects in Africa and China. "What about South America?" I asked. He went on to tell me that they didn't have anything going on yet in South America but that they were sending a team on a "vision trip" that year. I asked where, and he responded, "Colombia."

Intrigued, I then asked the pastor where in Colombia. He said that they would be visiting a small city in the middle of the Amazon jungle. He didn't name it. He was certain that I had not heard of the city. I continued to push for the name of the city, though, and finally he said, "Leticia." Shannon and I just laughed. God was leading. We would be joining this church.

The church was in transition, trying to find a new pastor, so I quickly found myself on the Pastor Search Committee helping find the next leader. Having gone through the difficult transition at Bellevue, Shannon and I did not want anything to do with a church in transition; we wanted to be settled. However, God had led us here, so we were obedient. I was honored to be part of the search committee, and God led us to an awesome, dynamic leader for the church.

Over the couple of years we were at this church, we developed great relationships. I was able to lead a few trips to Leticia to visit the orphanage and a missionary family who lived in the jungle and were from, of all places, Northwest Arkansas.

We were introduced to the family when we joined the church. As it turned out, I had actually met the wife when I led one of the Memphis teams to Colombia a few years earlier. What is more interesting is that they have four children, three of them the same ages as our kids. Our kids have become great friends over the years, and the couple remain two of our dearest friends in the world. I often wonder if we had moved to Colombia how our life might have been, living in community with this family.

So, needless to say, this church was a definite blessing in our lives, but Shannon and I concluded that life in Arkansas would forever be different for us. Deep relationships like we had in Memphis may never form again, and we were okay with that. We still had those relationships that we treasured. For our kids, though, they only know Arkansas. They ended up attending a local school and developing great relationships. They never looked back.

The Brevity of Life

Lest the point be forgotten, let me repeat: the season of renewal was not easy for my family. We dealt with the rough patches of loneliness, but in addition to that, we were handed multiple pictures of the brevity of life. Everyone passes through this stage, when family members reach the end of their journeys. Some may face it early in life, some late in life. But, the absolute truth is that life is short and those you care most about will not be around forever. Never put your hope in others, as this anchor will never hold.

I recognize many at this stage in life lose loved ones, but our losses seemed to come fast, and they came at a time when we were struggling to find footing in a new culture. Our family was hit with a number of deaths over our first few years in Arkansas.

During our first year in Arkansas, Shannon's mom, after battling a long illness, passed away. Shannon was able to be by her side in her last moments. This was tough on her, especially on top of the move. We traveled to Jefferson City, Missouri for the funeral, and my kids began to see the other side of life. I remember that the service was a clear presentation of the gospel, which is my hope for every funeral service. I pray I helped Shannon walk through that process okay, because I had no idea what I was in for in the coming year.

Back in Mississippi, my dad was not doing well. After battling and beating prostate cancer, he was diagnosed with Parkinson's disease, a cruel disease that slowly takes your mobility and mind. The heavy drugs used to treat his "park," as my dad fondly called it, really caused my father to become a different person. He hallucinated and had little energy. In fact, once, Dad fell asleep driving, careening off the side of the road, barreling through the woods, barely escaping death. After that accident, his back would never be the same. I watched his health deteriorate from Arkansas.

For a while, things became peaceful again. On the professional front, as we approached the first anniversary of our move to Northwest Arkansas, my job was going great. The company was small and entrepreneurial. I was used to large, multi-national companies where my success didn't exactly move the bottom line, but here, each of our performances tremendously impacted the company. We were all going after the same mission, living our values, and working to be a blessing to the world.

As the business continued to grow, I became a leader in the company. I became more and more committed to what we were doing, and God was clearly blessing our endeavors. As with most jobs, the company became a bigger piece of my and Shannon's life, everything that I thought it would be when I made the decision in Memphis. The company was an immeasurable blessing from God. I reflect on Joel 2:25 that says, "I will restore to you the years that the swarming locust has eaten" (NKJV). He did.

The kids were loving Arkansas. Riley was on the POM squad, Natalie was into dance, and Griffin was going after any sport that had a ball. The majority of family time was spent at the children's activities and school events. These were incredibly fun but incredibly busy times.

This stage of life, at least partially, explains the difficulty we had in growing relationship roots in Arkansas. We were doing life with other people traveling at the same speed—a speed at which it becomes hard to invest time in anything outside of your kids and marriage.

Then, everything came to a sudden stop. On November 29, 2014, at about 5:00 a.m., my cell phone rang. I didn't hear it, so Mom left me a brief, frantic message. She then called Shannon's cell, and, thank God, my wife answered it. My mom told Shannon to immediately hand the phone to me.

Waking up out of a deep sleep, I heard my mom describe the scene to me. Dad was lying on the floor. She thought that he had a heart attack. She explained frantically that she had called the ambulance. The paramedics were now walking in the house, and she needed to know if she should have them resuscitate Dad. I asked how long he had been unconscious, and she guessed about five minutes. I told her to let him go. Hardest phone call I have ever taken. Hardest decision I have ever made. Hardest moment of my life. Later my mom would question that decision, but she found peace in both of my brothers' saying that Dad had told them never to resuscitate.

As Dad lay motionless on the floor of their bedroom, right behind the ambulance, one of my nieces arrived. My niece said that she found Mom at Dad's side crying and telling him, "Don't leave me. I want to go too." Like the Bible says, husband and wife were one.

My mom cared for Dad's every move until his last day. In fact, as they prepared my dad for burial, they asked Mom if she wanted Dad's wedding ring. She told them to leave it on his finger, as he had never taken it off. That was her husband of fifty-two years. What a cool picture of the unity in marriage.

My father was loved by so many. During the night of the visitation, the extended family was gathered around his coffin, weeping. The pastors didn't seem to be leading the situation well, so I stepped in and asked everyone in the room if I could say a prayer. I remember praying a prayer of gratitude for what a great man Dad was. I said something along the lines of, "Some called him brother, one called him husband, some called him Poppy, and some called him friend. I had the pleasure of calling him Dad, and for that, I will be forever grateful. I thank God for giving me such a loving father. He would no doubt have died for me."

Growing up, my dad was my hero. I could always count on him to have my back. Dad taught me so much, about everything from religion to fishing to having a great work ethic. He taught me discipline and the fact that nothing would be given to me for free in life. He taught me how to compete, never settle. He always wanted the best for me and never wanted to see me struggle with life.

Dad had a tough time when I told him that I would leave my job in Memphis to do the work in Colombia, and as a dad myself, I can understand that. He saw how my life was being blessed financially and professionally and felt that I should stay in that position. Through all the twists and turns of my life, though, I had no greater supporter. I am forever grateful to Dad. I miss him and would give anything to have a conversation with him as a young, healthy man. I will one day.

The funeral was a military procession, with a gun salute and the playing of taps. It was a moving ceremony. Most interesting was the train roaring through as the pastor spoke, right as we were lowering Dad in the ground. The engine was almost Dad himself, powerfully exclaiming, as I know he would have, "Carry on!" Dad was a believer in Jesus, so he is carrying on too, feeling a whole lot better right now. Hope in God gets you through. Dad had an anchor that is still holding him today.

As we were finishing up this scene, caring for my mom, we received a call from Jefferson City, Missouri. Shannon's grandmother had taken a turn for the worse. We were told that they didn't think she would make it much longer. We immediately hit the road from Mississippi to Missouri, trying to make it before she passed away. Life, and death, was moving at Mach speed.

We barely made it to Missouri. As we entered Shannon's grandmother's house, Shannon and Natalie walked in her bedroom to see her hanging on. It was as if she'd waited for us to get there. She gasped, taking her final breath, and went to sleep. We huddled around the room and prayed.

We decided to hang around Jefferson City so Shannon could help the family get her grandmother's house in order. The kids and I only made a quick trip back to Arkansas to grab clothes for the funeral and a few other things and then returned to Jefferson City.

Shannon's grandmother lived a long life, dying at the age of ninety-two. She was married to the same man for sixty years, and as he battled cancer, she loved him, cared for him, until the end. They truly were a picture, a model, of marriage for our culture today. Again, two became one.

Shannon was close to her grandmother, who lovingly called her Shanny. People used to talk about how Shannon was her favorite grandchild, and I could tell when I was around them that they had a special connection. What a gift to have this special relationship with your grandmother—an opportunity that was slowly evaporating before my kids' eyes.

After the funeral, we traveled back to Northwest Arkansas, emotionally exhausted by the funerals and deaths we had experienced over the last month. My kids were learning a lot about life. I was learning a lot about life. As the Bible says, it is short; it is a mist, a vapor (Jas. 4:14).

Having now gained a good familiarity with Northwest Arkansas, we moved into a new house. From this house, we would be but a couple of miles from grocery stores, our church, the kids' school, my office, an amphitheater, great restaurants, shopping, you name it. We felt so blessed and jumped eagerly into our lives here.

But then, soon after, out of the blue, we received *another* call. Like a boxer who receives a right hook, falls to the floor, and, after struggling to get back to his feet, gets hit again, such was our family. The call was from Shannon's brother in middle Arkansas. Shannon's dad had been in a motorcycle accident. Knowledge of the extent of the injuries began coming in over the next hour.

Shannon's dad had been transported to a hospital in Little Rock. He had not been wearing his helmet, which he always wore, when a car pulled out in front of him. He laid the bike down and slid into the vehicle. Amazingly, we were told everything was going to be okay. He was beat-up pretty badly but would make it without long-term injuries.

We drove to see him that day, and he looked like he was in bad shape, as most do after a wreck. The great news, though, per the doctors, was that he had no brain injuries. We gathered with the family, prayed, and thanked God for caring for him. After a couple of days, we drove back home, staying in touch with the family, keeping close to the situation. Everything seemed to be progressing well.

But a few days later, Shannon got a call from her brother. I remember our whole family was there, gathered in the kitchen, watching Shannon's face turn from happiness to horror. She sat down, absorbing the news, then relayed what she had heard. Her dad had taken a turn for the worse, and it didn't appear that he was going to make it. Shannon immediately jumped in the car and drove down to be with him, while I stayed back with the kids.

Before Shannon could get to Little Rock, her dad died. Unbelievable. We were all stunned. How could things have gone from great to death in twenty-four hours? We all struggled with that turn of events, just resting in the sovereignty of God. Shannon and her siblings held together strong during this period, a testimony of their dad's love for them all.

Mr. Kenney seemed to have been taken too early. He was in great shape. He loved his family and grandkids so much and found great joy in having the family together. Since we moved to Arkansas, he had been getting closer to our kids and becoming more of a presence in our lives.

It was a tough blow for us all, but especially Shannon. This was actually the sixth death in her family since our move. In total, we lost seven members of our combined families. Everyone will deal with these heartaches at some point in life; however, you just don't expect them to come as quickly as ours did. No doubt, the Harvey's, kids included, faced a lot of hardship in dealing with these losses.

Home

After the funeral for Shannon's father, we arrived back to our home in Arkansas a different family, resolved to do our best to solidify the new life we had been creating. Northwest Arkansas became our home. Shannon and I saw that it was an incredible place to raise a family, and in fact, after some time, we could scarcely think of any place better. The area is full of things to do, safe, and blessed beyond belief. With the Walmart, Tyson, and JB Hunt headquarters all located in the area, the local economy is robust and growing dramatically each year.

However, these blessings come with a danger. As I have mentioned already, Jesus talked more about the danger of money than any other worldly pitfall. In Memphis, our friends and the people we were around were from different social classes. We had friends at all levels, and there didn't seem to be comparisons or a materiality mindset. Northwest Arkansas is a bit of a bubble, though. Sure, there are different classes, but those in the upper class, as a percentage, are much greater. The area has much wealth, and with that comes the real danger of getting caught up in trying to find your joy and happiness on this earth, which will never happen.

The danger of placing love in money is a risk for everyone, but especially for us in Northwest Arkansas. I will always have a deep love for the area, though, because I have seen God use Northwest Arkansas as a place of blessings for my family and many other people.

Arkansas is where we still reside as of the time of writing. Games, practices, business travel, and other activities keep us moving at a frantic pace. Other family members see it when they visit us. To quote Ferris Bueller, "Life moves pretty fast. If you don't stop and look around once in a while, you could miss it."[4]

We love Northwest Arkansas and continue to be blessed beyond belief. But, no doubt, life hasn't been the same as in Memphis. Our memories of Memphis—our marriage, the birth of our kids, the fellowship we experienced, our great friends—are all full of joy and nothing but. So far, for our short stint in Arkansas, our memories don't match up to the fond thoughts of yesteryear, and I'm not sure they ever will. I suppose that is the way life is.

Early on, I wrote about my parents speaking of the coast in Mississippi. They had fond memories of growing our family in this area. The coast was their Memphis. So, rest assured, the Harvey's love Arkansas, but we will always speak of our Memphis roots with great fondness.

The truth is, God is the same in Memphis, Arkansas, and Colombia. We have a tendency to make the journey of life about ourselves. We try to fit God into our precisely planned lives. However, God is the orchestrator of the journey. When we view the world through his eyes, we understand that he is at work the whole time. He directed us to an amazing area with great opportunities and people. When I step back and view the totality of the journey, I am only thankful for how he has led us, protected us, and brought us to Arkansas. God is indeed good.

Threads from the Renewal Season

The word *renewal* means "to make like new...restore to freshness, vigor, or perfection."[5] No doubt, this was a season of renewal. However, renewal for the Harvey's was anything but easy. The journey has been difficult but blessed.

The thing about renewal is that the season doesn't change who you are at your core or your past. Your old threads arrive with you and continue to weave as you navigate the twists and turns of the new season. The threads are permanent placements in your soul. The key to journeying well is how you manage them. Know them and steer them well.

There are also new threads that emerge during this season, though. For me, probably the biggest new thread is what I call maturity. The Bible speaks of spiritual maturity coming as one understands God more. I gained a deeper understanding of my Father. Things change, but he remains the same.

Spiritual maturity only comes from spending time with God, mainly in his Word. In spending time with him, one begins to understand more and more of his character. The more I walk with God, the more I understand, the more I love, the more I realize how I need him.

Left to my own thoughts and opinions, void of Scripture, I twist religion and the character of God into how I think it should be. I try to make sense of things through my view of the world. God is God, though. He created all. His ways are not my ways. This side of heaven, I will never completely understand his sovereignty. But, I understand more of his love for me after growing in spiritual maturity in my renewal season.

Another thread I picked up—or really, refined—was the thread of adaptability. After spending fifteen years in a place that is home, one must be incredibility adaptable to take on a new culture. Church is not the same, people are not the same, your life is not the same. During the renewal season, I learned not to fight the cultural difference but understand it, embrace it.

And then there is what is perhaps the sweetest part of a renewal season: the time it allows you to catch your breath and view your tapestry, your journey, with clarity. When the speed, confusion, and stress clear, you realize that God was walking with you the whole time. You turn around and see that the path you have been walking is illuminated. I suppose this is when you understand the value of the anchor. You see how God controlled the entire journey and how your threads have come together to form a magnificent picture.

Though the ship rocks at times in the rough sea, the anchor holds.

Reflect on your Season 5

For personal reflection, answer these questions about your journey.

- What are the 3 to 5 decisions that most impacted your life during this season?
- Who are the 5 people that had the biggest positive impact on your life?
- How did previous seasons impact season 5?
  - ○ How did the beliefs on religion and God play out in season 5?
  - ○ How did your view of people from previous seasons impact you in season 5?
  - ○ How did the areas where you have lived impact your journey in season 5?
- What storms came into your life and describe the impact of these storms.
- What threads were developed?
- List evidence of God's grace in your life during this season.
- What was your anchor during this season?
- Looking over this season, what are 3 pieces of advice you give your family, friends, the world.

Name this season in your life.

For a detailed format to record your journey, check out the Seasons Journal.

Reflection

But one thing I do: Forgetting what is behind and straining
toward what is ahead

PHILIPPIANS 3:13

As I walked into my new church this morning, I saw new faces. New people greeted me, and a new community awaited. None knew the threads woven into my fabric, my journey, or my life perspective, and I didn't know theirs. I only knew I was among individuals who each had threads, each had traveled a journey unknown to the outside world. I wondered what the world, this church, our class would look like if we took off the masks and let others see our tapestries.

One thing I know all of our tapestries would show: the only anchor in life that holds is God. And the way to understand and stay connected to the anchor is through his Word. Life offers no other stability.

As I finish the story about our lives up to this point, I am not sure what God has in store in the future for the Harvey's. I only know that God himself is with us, a promise he gave us in Matthew 28:20. There is great, unsurpassed peace in that verse. I couldn't live without it, as I know he has forgiven much.

The Bible tells the story of a man named Simon. Simon was a fisherman, the sea his hunting ground. One day, as he was pulling his net in on the beach by the Sea of Galilee, Jesus approached him, looking deep into his eyes. The Bible uses the Greek word *emblepo* to describe the gaze. *Emblepo* means to "look upon" with a "close, penetrating 'look.'"[6] Jesus, being God himself, looked at Simon and knew all that would happen in his life. He knew that Simon would say that he was committed but turn his back on him at his darkest hour. He knew that Simon's passion and tendencies to speak his mind would get him in trouble throughout his life. And he knew that Simon would never, could never, live a life without failure.

Yet, even knowing all of these shortcomings, Jesus didn't

condemn or pass Simon by to find someone who could better measure up. Not Jesus. Not him who was grace himself. Instead, at that moment, looking in his eyes, Jesus changed Simon's name to Peter, meaning "rock." At that moment, Jesus said that Peter would be a rock for his ministry, the church. Jesus overlooked the failures of Simon and welcomed the man Peter with open arms, giving him a life of immeasurable purpose, joy, and hope. In a moment, Peter's life changed forever.

And so it is with me. Like Peter, my life is full of failures and shortcomings. However, when Jesus first gazed into my eyes, he knew that. He knew my life would never measure up. It couldn't. But, he came to me anyway. Like Peter, I was given grace, and because of his grace, I am compelled to follow.

There is an awesome scene in the Bible that illustrates the grace of Jesus and the love he has for us, despite our shortcomings. As Jesus foreknew, Peter's final act toward him prior to his death was betrayal. As Jesus was getting brutally beaten and murdered, Peter refused to help. Worse, he pretended that he did not know him.

After the crucifixion of Jesus, when Mary went to the tomb early Sunday morning, the stone has been rolled away and there was an angel greeting her. Mary must have been startled beyond belief. She looked on in amazement. Jesus had risen! Everything he said was true!

Mark 16:7 captures the heart of Jesus. The angel turned to Mary and said, "Go, tell his disciples *and Peter*" (author's emphasis). Go and tell Peter. The one who had denied him and refused to acknowledge him. The one who was certainly hurting more than anyone else because he had turned his back on Jesus. The angel said to make sure Peter knew that Jesus had risen. Jesus cared for Peter and wanted him to know that everything was okay. "Forget about the sins, Peter. Just know that I have risen."

After receiving the news, Peter recklessly told others. As Jesus said in Luke 7:47, Peter had been forgiven much, so he loved Jesus much.

Again, the same is true in my life. As you read my story, you see that I have been forgiven much. Thank God for a Christ who overlooks it all and clears my guilt. He who has been forgiven much loves much. This, my friends, is the definition of grace. May it be true in your life as well.

The anchor holds.

The Anchor in Action

An anchor provides peace of mind, surety, stability, calmness in the midst of the storm. However, the ultimate role of an anchor is not to keep the vessel still, unmoving. Perhaps the greatest role of the anchor is the peace of mind it gives just from knowing that it is present. With an anchor aboard the ship, the vessel can freely travel, knowing the anchor is always available. The anchor provides freedom to go. After all, what value would an anchor have if the vessel never moved?

And so it is with the anchor of your soul. The anchor gives you freedom to go. Uncertainty is an absolute truth of the world. An anchor gives you peace to move forward when doubt and fear are all around.

Cherish your anchor.

9 *Lessons*

My journey has involved adventure, risk, folly, and forgiveness. More than anything, I want my kids to capture what I learned only later in life. I want them to recognize the value of knowing and following a holy God early in their walks so they don't have to experience the folly of youth, as Solomon says. With that, I will share some lessons that I want my kids to recognize early on, which I believe others can benefit from as well.

Lesson 1: Read and know the Bible.

Every bit of advice that I now give anyone begins with Scripture. The Bible is the lens through which I view the world. This lens will never lead you astray. The world, our culture, will constantly push against the words in the Bible, challenge those words. But, the words of God stand the test of time. The words of God are true. A life lived with this lens is a life of joy.

Lesson 2: Love the Jesus of the Bible.

The Bible is a book about your Savior. Many in the Bible knew the Scriptures without knowing the Savior. Develop a personal passion for Jesus that will fuel your life, your love for others. All other fires will be extinguished. This fire will remain forever.

Lesson 3: Understand the personal threads woven into your fabric.

As you have seen in my life, you are made up of threads from your heritage and history. Embrace these threads. This is how God made you, the life he gave you. Do not only embrace them, though. Know the threads intimately, because each one has positive and negative attributes. Know them enough to accentuate the positive and beware the negative. God gave you the negative as a warning.

Lesson 4: Cherish relationships, family and friends.

God gave us relationships as a gift. Recognize this. Don't take relationships for granted. When the going gets tough, you need people in your life who love you. Write a note to someone close to you today.

Lesson 5: Don't make mountains out of molehills.

Don't let the small issues of life become big issues. Let the molehills remain molehills. There are going to be some major issues in your journey. Times will come that rock your world. Storms will come that challenge your faith. As Adrian Rogers used to say, "You are either headed to a storm, in a storm, or coming out of a storm." Take the small issues in stride so that you have energy for the big ones.

Lesson 6: Control money; don't let it control you.

Jesus warned of money. He knew the danger that loomed with materiality. Recognize money as a gift and manage it wisely. Always be a giver, not one who goes after things.

Lesson 7: Don't judge others.

In our culture today, the focus of many a conversation is other people. We eat people for lunch. God, however, is the only judge. Learn from my life that everyone messes up. We are not the ones to point fingers, call people out. We are ones who love, no matter what.

Lesson 8: Fear is a trigger for action, a sign to move forward, to follow God and push through.

Never let fear stop you from doing. In fact, if you fear something, go after it hard. When you do, doors will open and you will see the world differently. God will lead you to places you never imagined. When you feel fear, recognize it and follow it.

Lesson 9: Don't follow culture; follow God.

God has a unique plan for your life. Culture will tell you otherwise, but don't copy it. Lean on Romans 12:2 to discover his will for your life. Then, recklessly go after it. You go after it, and let him provide the safety. Culture calls. So does Jesus.

Follow him.

Nine lessons. Nail them on your door post. Live them and you will live well.

A Parting Word about the Anchor

The quality of anything in my life is directly proportional to my biblical literacy.

I like to read. Look in my briefcase at any given time and you will find a couple of nonfiction business books. I don't read just anything, though. I feel that if I am going to invest time in reading, I need to get something out of it. That's just me.

Without exception, I believe the most underutilized, under-appreciated book is the Bible. Whether you are a Christian, an atheist, a believer in God, whatever, the Bible is an invaluable resource for history, a view of mankind. It is a literary master-piece. As an avid reader of the Bible, I have learned how the practical advice of this book will lead one to a successful, rich life.

A great example is the book of Ecclesiastes in the Bible, an autobiography written by King Solomon. Who would not cherish the insight of the wealthiest man on earth during his time, the King of Israel, an architect, an entrepreneur, a man with unsurpassed wisdom? Recounting his days, he describes his business accomplishments, his wealth, as nothing but "vanity" (Ecc. 1:2 ESV). Solomon found what we describe as success in the world to be nothing but vanity once acquired. In our day, how many times have you heard those who seemingly have it all describe life as empty? We run, we search, we acquire, only to find that everything is vanity. Solomon told us this truth before we ever started the race.

No doubt, Ecclesiastes is a rich book of insight that our society leaves to gather dust. And, the Bible is full of sixty-six books like Ecclesiastes.

Unfortunately, our culture has turned the Bible into a book that divides, that is full of friction. My challenge to people is to pick the book up and see what it says for yourself. The book is an underutilized gift that I discovered later in life. No matter your stage of life, wisdom of the Bible awaits.

Endnotes

1. Southeastern Conference (SEC), "It Just Means More," advertisement aired on ABC, September 2, 2017, 1 minute.

2. J.R.R. Tolkien, *The Fellowship of the Ring* (New York: Houghton Mifflin Company, 1994): 213.

3. The Grateful Dead, "Truckin'," recorded September 1970, track 10 on *American Beauty*, Warner Bros. Records, vinyl LP.

4. John Hughes, Tom Jacobson, Matthew Broderick, Alan Ruck, Mia Sara, Jeffrey Jones, Jennifer Grey, et al., *Ferris Bueller's Day Off.* (Hollywood: Paramount Pictures Corp., 1987).

5. *Merrian-Webster.com*, s.v. "Renew," accessed April 17, 2020, merriam-webster.com/dictionary/renew.

6. W.E. Vine, "Look – Vine's Expository Dictionary of New Testament Words," *Blue Letter Bible*, accessed April 17, 2020, blueletterbible.org/search/dictionary/viewTopic. cfm

About the Author

Mike lives in Northwest, AR, with his beautiful wife and three awesome kids. He is on the journey with all of you, desiring to leave a legacy for his kids and future generations. Ultimately, God's grace changed his life. His prayer is the same for you.

Reach Mike at impactothers.blog.